SAINT VINCENT DE PAUL

A short life of
Saint Vincent de Paul

by
Luigi Mezzadri C.M.

Translated by
Thomas Davitt C.M.

THE COLUMBA PRESS

First edition, 1992. This edition 2010 published by
THE COLUMBA PRESS
55A Spruce Avenue, Stillorgan Industrial Park,
Blackrock, Co Dublin

Cover by Bill Bolger
*The cover photograph is of a statue of St Vincent
on the main staircase in
McNamara House, Castleknock College.
It was the gift of Fr Joseph Brady CM in 1896.*
Origination by The Columba Press
Printed in Ireland by ColourBooks Ltd, Dublin

ISBN 978-1-85607- 692-0

Originally published as
S. Vincenzo de' Paoli: Una vita spesa per gli altri
by Luigi Mezzadri, Edizioni Borla, Roma, 1989.

Contents

Translator's Preface

When Fr Mezzadri asked me to translate his book, he suggested that I should make any changes which I considered helpful for English-speaking readers, and in particular that I should expand what he had written in chapter IV about the missionaries St Vincent sent to Ireland and Scotland. I have done this and, in order to keep the chapter to a reasonable length, I abbreviated what he had written about the missions in Italy.

I have also added some words of explanation after the names of some continental people and places, and introduced a few extra dates for the sake of greater clarity.

Finally, where direct quotations are given from St Vincent's writings, I have added the volume number and page (e.g. VI 123), mainly for the benefit of members of his two communities. Quotations without such a reference are not found in the fourteen volumes of his works but are attributed to him in different biographies.

T. Davitt C.M.
Blackrock
Co. Dublin

CHAPTER I

Conversion

It was a very hard winter's day that Wednesday, January 25, 1617, the feast of the Conversion of St Paul. The priest who was to preach in Folleville church, near Amiens, was struck by the size of his congregation and didn't allow himself to be distracted by the beauty of the rennaissance sculptures in the apse, beneath which were the bodies, or rather the dust, of people of influence, awaiting final judgement. The preacher instead felt himself questioned and probed by eyes rimmed by hunger and hardship, waiting in hope.

Before beginning to speak he took a look inside himself, going over his past. He felt as they did, he could speak for them, he embodied their thoughts. He glanced at the tabernacle, and at the crucifix which leaned out above the pulpit. He didn't feel like adding God's anger to people who were already putting up with the anger of landlords and the rigours of a Picardy winter. He decided to get on their side, to be always for them, "to take the first step". For the priest in Folleville the step was a decision to consecrate his entire life in dedication to God and to other people. He was Vincent de Paul, born in Pouy (now re-named St Vincent de Paul) near Dax, in the south-west of France in the region known as the Landes, on 24th of April 1581. He was the third of six children.

His parents, Jean de Paul and Bertrande de Moras, thought he seemed a likely lad to go on for the priesthood. Not that he was better or more religious than other boys, or that religion was up

9

for discussion. For the country people of the Landes it was as natural as the shade of the oaks and the inrush of flood waters. Later on in life Vincent was to say: "If there is any true religion... it is among such people that it is to be found" (XI 200). For the moment, though, it is not a question of faith or vocation but rather of a job and the family's future. Should the boy, in fact, become a priest, then he would be guaranteeing comfortable support for the entire household.

We may wonder how the saint's social background influenced him. He always kept the outlook of "a man from down the country" on the world and on things in general, even spiritual matters; Vincent's understanding of scripture is typical of a countryman. The quotation he chose as his programme is that passage of Luke in which Christ, in the Nazareth synagogue, announces that he has been sent to preach the gospel to the poor (Lk 4:18). The crest of the Congregation of the Mission, known as The Vincentians, shows a Christ who travels around preaching to the poor, against a background of the countryside. In contrast to other reformers of the Church in France, who were from the nobility, he always insisted on the importance of work. His religious outlook was not the drawing-room piety of those criticised in Molière's play *Tartuffe*, precisely because he appreciated the worth of work-worn hands, and the silent prayer of sweat and exhaustion. He had no wish to surround himself with intellectuals, or to take on the spiritual direction of cloistered nuns from the nobility. Poor himself, he chose the poor to evangelise the poor.

The memory of his mother and sisters probably played a large part, especially in the way he regarded women. There were few who valued the presence of women as he did, both in society and in the Church, at a time when their position was supposed to be one of submission, deprived of dignity, or confined to the role of the *précieuses*, always on the fringe.

From the age of fifteen he was at school with the Franciscans in Dax. From 1597 he continued his studies at the university of

Toulouse. If Vincent was short of money he was not short of initiative. He wanted to become a priest at any cost. Advance to ordination was rapid. On 13 September 1599 Vincent obtained dimissorial letters, for ordination to the priesthood, from the Vicar General of Dax. The new bishop of Dax, Jean-Jacques Dussault, appointed in 1598 and ordained bishop in 1599, had quickly shown himself to be a reforming bishop. Even if the decrees of the Council of Trent were not binding on the French bishops, he wanted them observed all the same. Perhaps Vincent wanted to take precautions against possible surprises, and to be sure of getting ordained, by going to an elderly bishop, François de Bourdeilles, bishop of Périgueux, who was confined to his castle of Château l'Evêque.

As there was no question of subterfuge it is rather worrying to see a student who puts himself forward for the priesthood. He calls himself, he is not called. He at once tried to get a parish, but there was a dispute about the one in question; he therefore headed off to Rome (probably in 1601). He was much impressed by the city.

He returned to his homeland and, with the determination of a true Gascon, set about looking for a position which, in a century where honour counted, would have to be an honourable one. He obtained the degree of Bachelor of Theology from the university of Toulouse and had the foolhardy idea that he might become a bishop.

As for carrying out any important project, money was needed; a lot of money. Providentially a small inheritance came his way, left to him by an old lady. He didn't find it easy to lay his hands on the money as it was in the form of a debt owed to his benefactress, and the debtor had fled. In order to collect what he was owed, Vincent set off in pursuit, and caught up with the fugitive in Marseilles. Having got his money he decided to start the return journey by boat.

The boat on which he was travelling was attacked by three

Turkish brigantines which were operating as privateers so the battle was not between equals. Vincent was wounded by an arrow and taken to Tunis as a slave. The saint then experienced the humiliation, not alone of being exposed for sale in the slave market, but also of being dependent on owners who in theory had absolute authority over him as if he were just a thing. He was bought by a fisherman, later on by an odd sort of doctor and finally by a renegade Christian. That's when his adventure reached its turning point. His owner had three wives. Two of them were well disposed towards the saint, one of them a Moslem. She was impressed when he sang psalms and the *Salve Regina*. She spoke of this to her husband and he began to feel nostalgia for his faith and his native land.

He and his slave made the northward journey across the sea and landed at Aigues Mortes. In France the roles were reversed. The slave was now in a position to help his owner, who was absolved. In recognition of what he had done, Vincent was allowed to accompany the papal vice-legate, Pietro Montorio, from Avignon back to Rome.

That's a lovely edifying story; perhaps just a bit too much so. That's why many historians have cast doubt on it. They have looked for reasons why Vincent might have wanted to cover up some of his past. Others have defended the account, as if it were a matter of defending the saint's reputation.

There could be a different solution; perhaps the fact, but not the account of it, is true. There are many accounts, from that period, of ships attacked, of men sold into slavery and their efforts to survive or escape. Taking everything into account, it is not impossible that the desire for freedom may have suggested to the two men to trust themselves to a fragile boat in search of liberty and, in the case of the owner, recovery of lost dignity.

At that time, Vincent was a man searching for himself, a Gascon who sought, in every way possible, to cut a fine figure. If the slavery affair had damaged him in the eyes of his benefactors, he had to recover lost time and, above all, lost reputation. That's why he fell back on the gift of story-telling which he had, and he embellished his disappearance with heart-rending and rather romantic details. He wrote two letters to a lawyer in Dax, who had helped him in his student days, giving an account of the slavery episode with the sort of details which make him out to be a saint.

Perhaps, though, things happened rather differently. A slave's life is made up of compromises; there can be heroics or adaptation to circumstances. Perhaps Vincent chose the second route, on the lookout for the right moment to flee. In that case, there is nothing of the hero, nothing showing the precocious saint.

Our idea is pure hypothesis, but it finds some support in a letter written to his mother about two years later. Writing home from Paris on the 17th of February 1610, Vincent admits a twofold objective: to do well for himself and his family:

> I'm annoyed that I still have to stay on in this city in order to re-activate my chances of advancement (which misfortune snatched from me) and can't therefore go back to you and help you in the way I should. But I have such hope in God's grace that he will bless my efforts and will soon give me the means of retiring honourably and spending the rest of my days with you (I 18).

For a priest, that is an admission of failure. Vincent therefore needed to change, to re-think his life, to give himself stronger motivation. He was in need of being converted.

In the autumn of 1608 he went to Paris. The first position he got in Paris was as one of the chaplains in charge of distributing alms on behalf of the former queen, Marguerite de Valois. She had been the first wife of Henri IV and had played a leading role in bringing about, a week after her marriage, the famous "night of blood", the massacre on St Bartholomew's night, 24 August 1572.

13

Vincent's principal work was giving out money or bread to the hundreds of poor people who came knocking at the door of the ex-queen's palace. He was giving hand-outs, not practising charity; he filled hands, not hearts. He was just making the system work; he had not undergone any real transformation.

At that time, Vincent's adviser was Pierre de Bérulle who, in November 1611, had just grouped together some priests, all persons of note, all with their doctorates in theology from the Sorbonne, all intending to live out the fullness of their priesthood. They wanted to be a community of priests, but not a religious order. Their ideal was the apostolic community of Jesus and his apostles. For this reason Bérulle and his companions wanted to be part of the "Order of Jesus", to be his "Oratory". They did not look for any positions or honours; all they aimed at was holiness. This was just the opposite of what Vincent had sought, so he did not join the Oratory.

However, he had some decisive interior experiences which purified him and changed him radically. At that time he was sharing lodgings with a man from his own part of the country. One day, when he was sick in bed, the chemist's messenger-boy delivered some medicine and, on the way out, pocketed a purse belonging to Vincent's fellow-lodger. When the owner of the money came back he demanded an explanation from Vincent about its absence. The patient could not come up with any realistic explanation and was therefore accused of being a thief. It was a terrible accusation for an ambitious man, one on the lookout for patrons. But at that point some sort of a change was taking place and Vincent decided to keep silent. Here is how he described the incident years later:

> There is somebody in the Congregation who, when accused of having robbed his companion, and when this false allegation was being spread around the house, preferred not to defend himself, and he used to reflect, seeing himself falsely accused: "Are you going to deny the accusation? You are accused of something which is not true. Oh,

no!", he exclaimed, turning to God, "I must put up with it patiently." And that's what he did (XI 337).

The incident had a happy outcome because the real culprit was discovered. But in the meantime Vincent had experienced the plight of the poor, the people who have no voice, people who have no one to stand up for them. This was the first time he did not run away.

Troubles in life never come singly. While he was with Queen Marguerite, he knew a theologian who confided to him that he was having fierce temptations against faith. Vincent tells the story this way:

> This doctor of theology ... finding himself in this horrible state, came to me to tell me that he was violently troubled by temptations against faith, that he had disgusting blasphemous thoughts against Jesus Christ, and also thoughts of despair even to the extent of feeling himself urged to throw himself out of a window ... His imagination was so blank, his mind so exhausted with making acts rejecting the temptations, that he could no longer do anything more. Having sunk to this wretched level he was advised to adopt a practice which consisted in this, that every time he pointed his hand or his finger towards the city of Rome, or towards some church, it would mean that he re-stated his belief in everything which the Roman Church believed. What eventually became of him? In the end God took pity on this unfortunate doctor. He fell ill and was suddenly freed from all his temptations. All at once the dark blindfold was removed from the eyes of his mind; he began to see all the truths of faith, and with such clarity that it seemed to him he could feel it or touch it with his hand (XI 32-34).

At this point it was Vincent's eyes which became clouded in dense darkness. He prayed, mortified himself but existed as if in

15

a gloomy night. He wrote out the articles of the creed and sewed them over his heart, like Pascal. Every time he felt tempted he used to place his hand over his heart, this gesture being his act of faith. In his previous trial he had experienced the situation of the poor who have no one to protect them. This time he was experiencing a more radical spiritual poverty, what Christ experienced on the cross, abandoned by God. Fine theology, faced with trials against faith, is incapable of meeting the cry of the unfortunate person who is tempted. This temptation lasted three to four years. Then Vincent took the resolution to start visiting the Charity Hospital founded by Queen Marie de Medici, who had invited the St John of God Brothers to come from Florence in 1601. The temptation disappeared. The poor had conquered and had freed him. From then on he would always be on their side. From then on he would realise that the best way to heal spiritual ills is to open people up to service of others.

Meanwhile he had been put in charge, in 1612, of the parish of Clichy, a village near Paris with a population of six hundred. He threw himself into this new experience with enthusiasm. The people were not used to priests like him, so a change came about. A lot of care was taken with the liturgy, and also with catechesis. As well as this, he established a sort of preparatory seminary which had a dozen youngsters, among them Antoine Portail, who was to be his first companion later on. When he was much older he was to say:

> I had a parish where people were so good and so obedient in doing everything I told them that, when I recommended them to go to confession on the first Sunday of each month, no one stayed away. They all used to come to confession and I would see, from day to day, the effect it had on their souls. I was so pleased with this, so consoled, that I used to say to myself: "My God, how happy I am to have such good people!" And I used to add: "I think the Pope would not be as happy as a Parish Priest in the midst of of such good-hearted people (IX 646).

The joy of pastoral life in Clichy did not last long. After one year there Vincent, on the advice of Bérulle, accepted the post of chaplain to an aristocratic family. The de Gondis were one of the families which counted for something in France at that time. They were bankers from Florence who had come to France with the Medicis. They had made their fortune and had become very influential through strategic marriages. They had acquired hereditary rights for family members to hold two important positions, commander of the galleys which were the French naval presence in the Mediterranean, and bishop of Paris. Philippe-Emmanuel de Gondi, the head of the family, was general of the galleys and the King's Lieutenant for the armies of the Levant; he also had the titles of Count of Joigny, Marquis of the Iles d'Or, Baron of Montmirail, Dampierre and Villepreux. His wife, Françoise-Marguerite de Silly, had brought him, as a dowry, the lordships of Enville, Commerey and Folleville. In this family's mansion Vincent was to be tutor and adviser, and his teaching affected the parents more than the children.

One day, Philippe-Emmanuel came to Vincent's Mass, having already committed himself to fighting a duel. He was asking God's help for a rash undertaking, as Vincent knew, so Vincent went down on his knees in front of him and said: "I know, from a reliable source, that you are thinking of fighting a duel. In the name of the God, whom I have held up before you and whom you have adored, I tell you that if you do not drop this evil plan he will make you and your family feel his justice." Philippe-Emmanuel accepted the concept of honour by which he felt bound, but Vincent's words pricked his conscience to such an extent that he abandoned his plan to fight the duel.

It was during his stay in the de Gondi household that Vincent experienced the radical turn-about in his life.

CHAPTER II

The Ambush

Many saints have been helped, or set on a certain path, by supernatural happenings. St Paul was thrown from his horse and heard the voice of Christ. The crucified Christ spoke to St Francis of Assisi in the church of San Damiano. St Ignatius of Loyola had an experience on the bank of the River Cardoner in which he was enlightened with a new awareness of, and insight into, the mysteries of the faith. St Paul of the Cross saw the Blessed Virgin wearing a black habit with a distinctive badge in the form of a cross, with the words: "The Passion of Jesus Christ."

By 1617, Vincent was already convinced that he had to go where God was leading him, and he accepted, or was resigned to, the fact that he should not expect to hear voices from above. Instead he had to follow more humdrum signs, the sort which we come up against in our everyday lives, ordinary circumstances and situations. He was not upset by this, but was like a man waiting in ambush, ready to lay hold of God's will in his life.

In January of 1617, Vincent was on the de Gondi estates in Picardy, in a village called Folleville, near Amiens, when he was called to the sickroom of one of the tenants, a man with a very good reputation. However, his general confession showed Vincent unbelievable spiritual misery. People were not going to confession and preferred, through shame, to keep silent about their spiritual troubles rather than unburden themselves of them. This was not just an isolated case; this was the general pattern all through France. The poor were not being evangelised or helped. Vincent knew that this was not through any shortage of priests; in fact there were too many, but they preferred to look after themselves and ensure their own welfare. Becoming a priest did not mean taking on fatiguing work and discomfort; it meant joining the "first order of the kingdom." This was just what Vincent himself had done.

The tenant in question felt that in his confession to Vincent he was understood and, feeling relieved, decided to tell Madame de Gondi about it. She was horrified and went to Vincent to see what could be done. She urged him to preach a sermon on general confessions. It was January 25, the feast of the Conversion of St Paul. He preached the sermon which has since become famous. The people got the message and besieged his confession box, and Vincent had to get help from another priest and some Jesuits.

With the passage of time Vincent came to realise that this was not merely a chance happening. He saw it as an encounter with God, where God showed him what he wanted him to do with his life. For this reason he always regarded the Folleville sermon as the first sermon of the Congregation of the Mission, though his Congregation had not yet been founded. But it was only later on that he came to see it in this way, because it was only very slowly that he became aware that he was being called to a type of evangelisation involving travelling around among the poor people in country areas.

At the time, the one thing clear to him was that he could not stay on in the de Gondi mansion because he felt more and more restricted, almost stifled, there. He went to Bérulle for advice, and Bérulle did not disapprove; but he did not have anything further to say, apart from indicating a place where he might be able to put his ideas of how to be a good Parish Priest into practice. This was the parish of Châtillon-les-Dombes, now called Châtillon-sur-Chalaronne, near Lyons.

This was a village only recently incorporated into France. The six priests there preferred the taverns to their prayers and, with that sort of example being given, the Catholic community was indifferent and the Calvinists thrived. Vincent's policy was to teach by example, and his first converts were the priests; that was the most difficult task. There was also an unrepentent duelling swordsman, the Count de Rougemont, whom he impressed. The count had the courage to shatter his sword on a rock, the sword with which he had won a hundred duels; he also sold part of his estates in order to build churches and help the poor. Finally, Vincent's Calvinist landlord became a Catholic, along with some of his nephews.

Another providential encounter was also approaching. On August 20 word was brought to Vincent just before Mass that there was a family which had nothing to eat because everyone was sick. Vincent decided there and then to change the theme of his sermon. What he said had its effect and the people willingly responded, and that afternoon a huge number went to help the family he had mentioned in his sermon.

He immediately realised that once-off sudden enthusiasm was not what was needed. Nothing further would be done unless there was some sort of organisation. Vincent had now come into contact with the other face of poverty, economic poverty, and he realised that neither the good neighbourliness of ordinary country people nor simple almsgiving was the solution. His opinion was that it was up to the Church to take on the fight against poverty, so he called a meeting of some of the local people. He suggested setting up a group to look after the sick poor of their village. They were all enthusiastic about the idea and Vincent drew up a set of rules, and that was the start of the Confraternities of Charity. They were groups based in parishes and they initiated a new insight into the Church as the setting in which charity is localised. 1617 is rightly considered as the decisive year for Vincent, the year in which his creative genius flowered.

It suited him to go back to Paris, to the de Gondis. After much insistence they had convinced him to return and resume his work, but with the freedom to travel around on his ministry of preaching. Vincent was in agreement. He was now mature enough to set up various works, perhaps even to establish religious communities, but his ordinary human qualities were not yet fully developed, nor had he a sufficient depth of spirituality, for real holiness. He had to face up to facts when Marguerite de Gondi, with the tact of an educated person and the sure touch of a soul close to God, showed amazement at his "black moods", his gloom.

He started preaching all over the de Gondi estates, giving missions and founding new Confraternities of Charity. In 1618 he started visiting the galley-slaves in Paris, and their pitiful state made a deep impression on him. Later on he told the Daughters of Charity: "I saw these people treated like animals" (X 125). He was not content with a mere token of sympathy. Charity teaches that we should share the problems of others, but also that relationships have to be re-built. There is a very significant incident mentioned in some of the early books about Vincent. In the course of one voyage he is supposed to have put himself at the oar in place of an exhausted galley-slave whose back was scored by the lash of the officer in charge. The story, of course, is not true; it's just a legend. But, as a matter of fact, it does not say enough; he did far more than that. Taking someone's place at an oar would not have achieved anything. Perhaps he did intervene once on behalf of some individual, but once he was back on shore things would have gone on as before, worse than before. He started doing something about getting better treatment for them, providing material and spiritual help for them, and succeeded in obtaining a new centre for them in Paris and a hospital for them in Marseilles.

Towards the end of 1618, the bishop of Geneva, Francis de Sales, arrived in Paris. He was welcomed by fashionable society with interest and curiosity. He did not behave like an actor playing a part. He came in order to convert, not just to be applauded and fawned on. On one occasion he simply told the story of the life of St Martin of Tours to a congregation which was expecting the fireworks of dazzling oratory. He also met Vincent, and told him about this incident. This was an important meeting for Vincent. He had to revise his scale of values. He realised that humility can bring happiness, overcoming personal pride. He opted for a life of humility, and in exchange God gave him the first signs of recognition: the bishop of Geneva and Jane Frances de Chantal entrusted to him the direction of the first monastery of the Visitation nuns in Paris. He also learnt the lesson of gentleness, a virtue which did not come naturally to him. When he saw this virtue in Francis de Sales he could not help reflecting: "How good you must be, my God, if Francis de Sales, your creature, is so gentle and lovable" (XIII 78).

He went back over what Madame de Gondi had said. It was true; he could not fool himself by saying he was made that way and could not change. He had a clear example right before his eyes in seeing how Francis de Sales and Jane Frances de Chantal got along with each other. This was an example of gentleness, but also of a holy friendliness between a man and a woman. He went on retreat to the Carthusian priory of Valprofonde, and then in Soissons.

At the priory he told a mature and holy monk about his personal problems in dealing with women. As an answer he was told a story. A bishop was not at his ease when baptising women and he asked God to be freed from temptation. But since nothing changed he went off into the desert where God let him see three crowns which had been prepared for him, each one more splendid than the previous one; because of his lack of trust he was to be allotted the least splendid one.

In Soissons he examined himself on his black moods, and on his hard aggressive nature. He asked God to help him to change. Making a retreat did not change him suddenly as if a magic wand had been waved over him. It helped him to understand the direction in which his priesthood should go and also the beauty of serving others.

In actual fact Vincent, coming to the end of ten years of searching for himself, now found nothing better than running himself down. This was a sign that he had not found himself, a sign that he had not yet found anything, a sign that he was still not a saint. That's why, after the breakthrough of 1617, Vincent still had to work through his problems, still had to search, especially to search for himself. Gradually his interior resistances caved in.

CHAPTER III

His flair is given its chance

Giving local missions to the people was what brought out Vincent's talent. He started preaching, but in a completely new way. He had been trained in the traditional way, and knew how to compose a talk with its various sections. There still exists a copy of a talk which Vincent composed in an oratorical style, which Fr Pierre Coste CM, who wrote an important biography of the saint, thinks was written in 1616. It is carefully composed, and even has a certain warmth about it. At the end there is an appeal to parents to send their children to catechism, and a carefully composed rhetorical flourish brings it to a close.

The change which took place in 1617 was along the lines of his re-discovery of priesthood. If up to 1608 he had considered the priesthood as the only chance in his life to obtain some sort of human affirmation for himself, it was after Clichy that he had come to appreciate the attraction of pastoral ministry and had gradually taken on the demands which the Council of Trent called for in a good priest. These demands were both interior and exterior, such as a spirit of prayer, a life of self-discipline, residence in the parish and the duty of putting into practice the methods laid down for pastoral ministry, namely preaching and the sacraments.

Events were now showing him that it was not enough just to go on the defensive. Many of the people of his own time saw Protestant opposition as the greatest danger to Catholic France. For this reason many preachers got involved in some form of bitter confrontation. A former member of a religious order admitted this in 1618. He said that often he would not allow Protestant ministers finish their sermon, but would launch into open debate. A glance at the situation in the countryside, on the other hand, showed Vincent that debating was not what was most needed; there was a need for God. While he was staying in the De Gondi mansion in Montmirail in 1620, he met a Protestant who made an objection which carried some weight. Vincent had stated that the Church was guided by the Holy Spirit. Facts, however, gave the lie to this:

> Look around the countryside. Priests are vicious, ignorant, without zeal. As a result the faithful are left without instruction, they don't even know what their duties are; and if they were asked what the Christian religion was, many would be hard put to it to answer. Now have a look at the cities. They are full of lazy priests and friars. In Paris alone there are supposed to be about ten thousand. While such priests are wasting their time the poor people down the country are being damned because of the state of ignorance in which they have been abandoned.

In the following year the Protestant was converted. When he saw Vincent leading a small band of priests, including the archdeacons of Chartres and Beauvais, for a mission in Marchais, near Montmirail, he gave in: "Now I see," he said, "that the Holy Spirit does guide the Roman Church." It was not Vincent's answers which brought this about, but his actions.

Vincent showed an extraordinary capacity for co-operation. He never acted on his own, but always looked for help from others and he had the gift of drawing out their talents. He was working for the Church; in a way, he was bringing the Church to birth.

There was need for this. The majority of the French population lived in rural areas. The Parish Priests had an important role in the preservation and growth of the faith, but they were in no condition to carry out this role. Vincent once said that the Church was on the road to ruin because of the bad life of priests, and it was they who would wreck and destroy it. A canon wrote to him:

> In this diocese the clergy are without discipline, the people without fear, the priests without either holiness or charity, the pulpits without preachers, knowledge is without honour and vice without punishment.

The churches were, in fact, in a lamentable state, with thatched roofs. There were tabernacles in which the hosts were crawling with worms and in which money or letters were often kept. The sacred vessels and vestments were filthy. Parish Priests in country areas were popular because of their weaknesses rather than their holiness, as, for example, when they were carried home drunk from taverns, or when they drew down reprimands on themselves for their attitude to chastity. If the figure of seven thousand priests who dishonoured their chastity, as mentioned in a letter to Vincent from a good canon, is an exaggeration, the fact is that in the diocese of Chartres one parish in every six gave reason for disapproval, and in the archdeaconry of Brie there was evidence of twenty licentious priests in a hundred and one parishes where canonical visitations had been made.

With regard to the administration of the sacraments the picture was even more gloomy. Vincent himself is on record as having seen seven or eight priests in St Germain-en-Laye who all celebrated Mass in different ways, each according to his own fashion (XII 258). And then there were priests who did not know the correct form of sacramental absolution in confession. By this time Vincent no longer needed any voices from above to understand God's will; what he saw was enough.

At the start of 1618 he was immersed in the awful conditions of the galley-slaves' prison. Imprisonment was not used by the state as a means of punishment for crime, but only as a method of detention for those awaiting trial. There were two types of severe sentence provided for, the death penalty and being condemned to the oars on the galleys. These were two different methods of killing. In the first case the sentence was public, ignominious, very theatrical, but was over and done with quickly. Being sentenced to the galleys was a prolonged death; it was hell. Later on Vincent was to say to the Daughters of Charity:

> Sisters, what happiness to be of service to the poor galley-slaves who are abandoned into the hands of merciless men! I have seen these unfortunates treated like animals (X 125).

He took the matter up with Philippe-Emmanuel de Gondi to get them treated in a more human way and he got a new centre established for them. In 1619 he was appointed chaplain-general of the galleys "for the benefit and advantage of the galley-slaves", the idea being " that they could profit spiritually from their physical punishment." While the flotilla of galleys was stationed in Bordeaux, so that they could take part in the exhausting siege of La Rochelle, Vincent got the idea of organising a mission for those condemned to the oars. He got help from priests of different religious orders. For many of the condemned men, a little chink of hope was opened up.

As soon as the mission was over Vincent thought of paying a visit to his relations, as Pouy was not very far from Bordeaux. He went on barefoot pilgrimage from the church of his birthplace to the Marian shrine of Buglose. He did not spend much time with his relations and he was sick at heart when he left. He was a man of forty-two who had accepted the reforms of the Council of Trent. Like the other reformers, he knew that one of the principal causes of the decadence of the later Middle Ages was that it had been forgotten that the Church's riches were "the blood of the poor." He told his relations that even if he had chests of silver and gold he would not have been able to give them anything "because a priest who possesses anything owes it to God and to the poor" (XII 219). This was a sacrosanct truth. Maybe none of his family asked him for anything, as his behaviour left no room for doubt; and there were no hopes either.

So, when the time came to leave, he was filled with sadness, since he knew they were poor. Some years later he admitted to his community:

> Fathers and Brothers, that's the state to which my relations were reduced: they needed alms; alms! (XI 329).

He could not, in conscience, do anything about it without betraying his convictions. He broke down in tears. And he took a long time to get over the remorse and sorrow, and thirty-six years later, on his deathbed, he he still remembered the taste of those tears. He could have stayed at home; he was someone who counted, he had good contacts and at that time he could have set his sights on some important position as a Parish Priest or canon. But he did not want to do this. He had to be rooted out from his native soil and, like Abraham, head off towards the new horizons of God. He had to be, and wanted to be, a missioner, so back he went to the preaching.

If, at the time of the Châtillon episode, Madame de Gondi was afraid of losing him, it was the other way around now. The noble lady had realised that she could not interfere with the generosity of this priest. If she had kept him with her, Vincent would have become a sort of hostage. In order not to lose him completely she had the idea of encouraging his plans and she gave her approval to the work of missions. As these were to take place on the various de Gondi estates it meant that she was still able to retain the services of her valued chaplain.

Madame de Gondi's backing was important for another reason also. Vincent well knew what conditions were like throughout the countryside. The people were extremely poor, most being reduced to struggling merely to exist. After his visit home, Vincent realised that from then on he would have to live without payment from the people to whom he ministered. Some founders of missionary communities, or famous preachers, preferred to rely on the generosity of the people, but Vincent was realistic and was afraid that this would be a burden on them. Madame de Gondi gave him the means to carry out his plan, by leaving him a large sum of money, the interest on which would take care of the expenses involved in giving missions (XIII 197). He was appointed rector of the Collège des Bons Enfants in Paris and this gave him something permanent and definite, an independent base. For him "countryman" meant possession of a house, the start of a family.

It was not difficult for him to find others prepared to share his enthusiasm. He looked around, and the first to take up his invitation was a young man whom he had influenced in Clichy, Antoine Portail. After leaving the parish Vincent had kept in touch with him. He had done his studies in the Sorbonne and had been ordained in 1622, and had great admiration for his former master. When Vincent took up his new post in the Bons Enfants, he sent for Portail and together with another priest they shared the joy of giving missions.

> The three of us used to go from village to village preaching and giving missions, and when we set out we'd give the key of the house to one of the neighbours and ask him to sleep in the house at night ... I had only one sermon, which I adapted in a thousand ways, on the fear of God" (XII 8).

Vincent was the only one who preached, as Portail was too timid and was afraid to face people. He used to keep in Vincent's shadow, and was to do so for a long time (I 88). Jean de la Salle and François du Coudray joined them. When they got the approval of the archbishop of Paris, they made a pilgrimage on foot to Montmartre to ask for the grace of not having anything other than God, and of doing everything for God.

CHAPTER IV

Together like brothers

Things were not simple at the start. The original idea was complex and contained the essentials of its later development; it was a seed for the future. Missioners who wanted to join Vincent had to commit themselves to working for the salvation of the poor people in rural areas. To reduce this to practice the founder asked for life in common, obedience, giving up benefices or positions in the Church, preaching missions without looking for payment and never in the cathedral town of a diocese, and working for the galley-slaves. Every so often there were days of recollection, days for "re-charging" with a view to further missions (XIII 197 ff).

What Vincent proposed was very demanding. It meant getting very tired and having to do without many things. After his ten years of escapism, of searching for a respectable way of supporting himself, Vincent had faced up to the beauty of his priesthood, because he had discovered Christ and seen himself in a new light. A little over a year before his death he said, in a talk to his community:

> We are chosen by God as instruments of his immense fatherly love which wants to root itself in, and spread through, souls ...That means our vocation is to go not merely to one parish or even one diocese but all over the earth. And to do what? To inflame men's hearts to do what the Son of God did. He came to bring fire to the earth by inflaming it with his love. What else can we want except that it burns and consumes everything? (XII 262).

The lure of the apostolic life was stronger than any fear. It was not long until other priests came knocking at the door of the Collège des Bons Enfants. In 1631 it had seven, and gradually the place became too small for the increasing numbers. In 1638 the first two Irishmen joined Vincent's Congregation, John Skyddie and James Water, both from Cork. By Vincent's death in 1660, twenty-three Irishmen had joined, as well as two Scotsmen and a Jerseyman. (The first Englishman did not join until 1744).

Problems greater than mere shortage of accommodation soon arrived, from Rome. At the start the new community was merely a "mission", a group of priests who had come together to carry on a certain apostolate. It got its first approval from the Congregation for the Propagation of the Faith, founded in 1622 by Pope Gregory XV. A further effort to get wider powers failed (XIII 225). There was a fear in Rome that Vincent wanted to found a religious congregation and that, with the passage of time, this might succumb to the temptation to abandon the difficult apostolate of the countryside and build itself comfortable houses in towns. There were in fact many members of religious communities in France who saw their vocation more in terms of their own salvation than of evangelising.

Vincent was not looking for privileges from Rome; he was looking for some guarantee that would hold the team together for the service of the poor. In 1631 he wrote to François du Coudray, one of his priests whom he had sent to Rome to deal with such matters:

> You must make them understand that the poor people are being damned because they do not know those things necessary for salvation and because they are not going to confession. If His Holiness knew the great need he would not give himself any rest until he had done all he could to rectify this.

And then he added five basic points: only bishops would determine the place where missions were to be given; while in a parish the missioners would be dependent on the Parish Priest; missions would be given without payment; missioners would not give missions in the cathedral town of a diocese; missioners would be dependent on the superiors of the congregation (I 115).

Meanwhile, though, something had changed. In July 1628 Vincent had been travelling with Augustin Potier, bishop of Beauvais. The day was hot and the journey was tiring. In spite of the jolting of the coach the bishop seemed to be dozing; in reality he was lost in thought. He grieved over the state of the Church and knew that in many ways it depended on the behaviour of the clergy; both of them were in agreement on this. Vincent had admitted that it seemed to him that a new beginning had to be made. Instead of an attempt to reform older priests, who had grown accustomed to a lifestyle which was far from spiritual, what was needed was attention to the new recruits. That's what the bishop was turning over in his mind. Suddenly he unexpectedly roused himself. He had hit on the solution: "I'll take them into my own house for a few days, and during that time they'll give themselves to prayer and will receive instruction in their duties and functions." It was a very simple idea, but practical and effective, and a provisional programme was drawn up. On 17 September 1628, in Beauvais, the first ever retreat for those preparing for ordination took place.

Today that might not seem very much. But at that time it was an important milepost. Up to then little attention had been given to the formation of priests, provided they could read and write, had some notion of ceremonies and some elementary learning. It was an apprenticeship; they learned things to do, not a way of life.

The success of the retreat in Beauvais led to similar ones being given in Paris. There was not room enough to accommodate all those wanting to come. Providence stepped in. Just north of Paris there was a huge priory which was in a run-down state because the monks of St Genevieve were unable to utilise all of it. The prior, Adrien Le Bon, offered it to Vincent. It was quite something. Even today if we take a look at a map of Paris we can appreciate the enormous extent of the property; it covered about ninety acres. But Vincent refused. He worked according to principles rather different from merely human prudence. In the end, though, he gave in and the contract for handing over the property was signed in January 1632. A year later the papal document, *Salvatoris nostri,* arrived from Rome setting out the legal basis of the community, and one of the stated purposes of the community was the formation of priests.

The headqaurters of the congregation was established in this priory, called St Lazare. From there the outreach towards people started. Further foundations were established in an impressive sequence, a sequence dictated by the call of God and not by the logic of human concerns.

In 1635 Vincent began sending out his men to establish new houses of his congregation; the first was in Toul in the province of Lorraine. Two years later another was opened in Aiguillon; this community later moved to Notre Dame de la Rose. Then in 1638 came Richelieu, Luçon and Troyes. The next year the missioners went outside the kingdom and opened a house in Annecy, in the Duchy of Savoy. Rome came next, in 1642, then Marseilles (1643). In 1645 he opened a house in Genoa, a house in which the missioners would have one of their most searing trials. In 1645-1646 it was the turn of Tunis and Algiers, and also an expedition to Ireland. Then came the heroic and tragic mission to Madagascar in 1648 (see chapter VIII). By now Vincent's heart and his courage went hand in hand; he did not seem to feel the weight of his years.

At the centre, in St Lazare, there was a really united community. In 1644 Vincent wrote to one of his priests about it:

> Such regularity, union and cordiality have never been seen before. It is like a small paradise (II 445).

The main work of the house was a ministry of welcome. Those who came for retreats were struck by it. Vincent himself commented that when the house had been a leper hospital it had been like a tomb, whereas now it was a place of resurrection (XI 16). A priest from Languedoc said he had never been so well looked after. He was welcomed by Vincent, and he was not treated as a stranger but with such love that he was really touched by it. During his retreat he thought he was in heaven, and when he left he did not feel that he was going to freedom but to prison. Many came in order to make a choice for their lives, and from there they took off like birds in a new direction.

The other houses of the Congregation were staffed by men who did not have talents which attracted attention, simple ordinary men, yet taken as a group they formed a community far from ordinary.

The missions were thriving; for Vincent they had absolute priority. In 1634 one of his missioners, François du Coudray, had the idea of making a Latin translation of the Syriac bible; Vincent was appalled. Just at that moment an urgent appeal came from a bishop asking for missioners to preach in the Cevennes. If du Coudray couldn't go then Vincent himself would have to go and work and die for a people "dying of hunger for the word of God" (I 249).

The results of the missions were almost unbelievable. In one place the church bells rang out for the sermon at two in the morning, and the church rapidly filled up. People queued up for confession, waiting for hours; sometimes they slept in the church or outside the doors. One of the missioners in Toul wrote back that in a whole month of work he did not have a single free day or a break. In Pleurtruit, in Brittany, there were five thousand general confessions. One gentleman knelt down in the graveyard and asked pardon of those he had offended. In Richelieu, during and after the mission, the people from the locality used to chant the litanies and the commandments.

In Italy the work of the missioners left very obvious traces and news of what they were accomplishing spread around. They were invited to other places. They would accept invitations to go where the problems were greatest, where others did not want to go.

Vincent was overjoyed at all this. The courage shown by his missioners prevented him from aging.

What was the secret of the missioners' lives? Above all was the founder's conviction that everything was the work of God. Vincent often said:

> Who called us to the missions, to pre-ordination retreats, to organising conferences for priests, to retreats for clergy and laity? Was it myself? No way! Was it Fr Portail, whom God sent to me right at the start? Definitely not, since we were not thinking that way nor making any plans. Who, then was responsible? It was God, his fatherly Providence and sheer goodness (XI 38).

If the Congregation was born from the heart of God then all its missioners should try to be like Christ in their thoughts, in their work and in their motivation (XII 75). Their vocation was, therefore, above all a way of life from which emerged "the five virtues". They are not just a list of qualities. They indicate a style, they make up a picture, they regulate a way of living.

In the first place Vincent asked his missioners for simplicity. They should be like the purest crystal filtering all the glory of God, and so doing everything for the love of God (XII 302). Next comes humility. In a century in which honour counted for so much, when people killed each other for an insult or for slighting a right of precedence, humility built up a strong personality, centred on God. The third virtue was gentleness. This was suggested to Vincent by the necessity of being with poor people. He did not want men proud of their learning, like professors straight from their studies. The people who swarmed around the confession boxes, who crowded together under the pulpit, were rough, ignorant, thick. They learnt more from goodness than from words, more from a caring tone of voice than from subtle arguments. Finally came self-discipline and enthusiasm for the gospel. For Vincent self-discipline did not mean constricting people, making them into mere prattlers in the presence of others, but rather removing the obstacles which blocked real freedom. And real liberty was something to be had only by someone who has ceased to resist the gospel, even to death; not physical death, but the death of love.

Take Etienne Blatiron, for example. He had been sent to Genoa and quickly showed unbelievable activity. In 1656 plague broke out. At once he put himself, with two of his confreres, at the disposal of the archbishop to care for the plague-stricken. Vincent reacted very positively to this: "There is no greater love than giving your life for others" (VI 58). When a request came for a chaplain for the Consolation Hospital, for lepers, Luca Arimondo volunteered; he made a retreat and left for the post. After twelve days of work and three of sickness he was mown down by the plague. But that was the first seed; he was very soon followed by others. Seven of the eight whom Vincent had sent to Genoa died. When he heard the news he summoned the community in St Lazare:

> Blatiron, who was a great servant of God, is dead ... Duport has also been taken by the plague ... Domenico Bocconi has also died in a hospital for the plague-stricken ... Tratebas, he's also dead. Vincent, too ... he's gone ... [Mc]Ennery, also dead (XI, 430, n.).

John McEnnery was a Limerickman.

Early death at work also claimed many others. Lambert aux Couteaux was forty-five when he was sent to Poland. The Queen, Louise-Marie de Gonzague, relied on him a lot. This lady, who knew how to fill the Polish court with her radiant beauty, was far from Paris and she wanted to have around her people who spoke her native French. Lambert, however, was made of the same stuff as Vincent. He gave himself unsparingly to the plague-stricken, first in Cracow and then in Warsaw. He organised, encouraged, and spent himself unstintingly, and exhaustion struck him down before illness. The Queen asked for another Lambert, and Vincent was at a loss what to do. He had ordinary men to choose from, not heroes. He sent Charles Ozenne, and when this ordinary man found himself in dangerous situations where he was needed he became a hero. He also died of exhaustion and sickness, aged forty-six.

He also sent ordinary men to Ireland and to the islands and highlands of Scotland. Cardinal Antonio Barberini, Prefect of the Congregation for the Propagation of the Faith, wrote to him on 25 February 1645, requesting him to send some of his men to Ireland (II 505). At home they were quiet, unobtrusive men, gentle and charitable. Enthusiasm for the gospel transformed them. They were all tireless men, going through wild regions, hunted all the time. Proof that they were priests was all that was needed to get them the death sentence.

A group of eight or nine left for Ireland in late 1646: Gerard Brin (from the diocese of Cashel), Dermot Duggan (Emly), Edmund Barry (Cloyne), Thady Lee (a seminarian from Limerick), a French priest, a French seminarian and a lay brother from Jersey. The names of the eighth and possible ninth members of the group are not certain, but George White (Limerick) and/or Dermot O'Brien (Emly) are likely. They gave missions in the dioceses of Cashel, Emly and Limerick. The two Frenchmen and the Jerseyman were ill most of the time and it was decided to send them back to France; one or two of the Irishmen probably went with them. It is certain that Frs Barry and Brin, and the seminarian Thady Lee, remained on in Ireland. They gave a mission in Limerick at the time of the siege of the city by the Cromwellian army under Ireton in 1651. In a letter to the superior in Warsaw, dated 22 March 1652, Vincent reports that Frs Brin and Barry escaped from Limerick. In a PS he adds:

37

Poor Brother Lye, while in his home area fell into the hands of his enemies; they bashed in his head and chopped off his hands and feet in the presence of his mother (IV 343).

Edmund O'Dwyer, bishop of Limerick, wrote to Vincent:

It is only right, Father, that I should thank you with all my heart for the benefit I received from you through your priests, and that I let you know the very great need we have of them in this country. I can confidently assure you that their work has produced better results, and that they have converted more people, than all the rest of the priests. And, what's more, because of their example and exemplary way of life the majority of the upper classes, of both sexes, have become models of virtue and devotion, which was certainly not the case before your missioners arrived in these parts (III 356-7).

The archbishop of Cashel, Thomas Walsh, also wrote to Vincent, in a rather stilted style:

The departure of your missioners gives me the opportunity of passing on to you my humble acknowledgement of, and gratitude for, the fact that, through your great charity, you consented to help, by your missionary priests, the little flock which God has committed to me … And although these good priests have had to put up with a lot of difficulties since their arrival in this country this did not prevent their giving themselves continuously, like tireless workers, to the work of their mission; with the help of grace they gloriously extended and increased the worship and glory of God (III 357).

After leaving Ireland, Dermot Duggan went to Scotland, working mainly in the Hebrides. Everywhere he went the Church was reborn, coming out into the light of the sun. On the islands of Eigg and Canna he converted eight or nine hundred people, while there were about twelve hundred conversions on Uist where before his arrival there had not been a single Catholic. He died there in 1657 aged thirty-seven.

Another Vincentian from Limerick, Francis White, also went on the Scottish mission, working mainly in the Highlands. He was captured while in the castle of the Marquis of Huntley. Proof that he had celebrated Mass would have cost him his head. Vincent was shattered, and he reported to his community in St Lazare: "Here's a fine missioner on his way to martyrdom" (XI 173). However, no one could furnish the necessary proof and White was released after a few months.

A Scottish Vincentian, Thomas Lumsden, from Aberdeen, one of two Scotsmen who joined the Congregation in Vincent's lifetime, also worked in his native land. In October 1657 he wrote back to Vincent about his work, saying he had to be vague about details in case the letter fell into the wrong hands. He mentions that he had ministered in "Moray, Ross, Sutherland, Candie and Caithness" and that he had also gone to the islands of Orkney (VI 531).

CHAPTER V

The Daughters of Charity

Vincent did not want the apostolate to be the exclusive domain of men. He wanted a single, common, compact front, so he involved women. Two groups played their part in bringing about this involvement. First came the Confraternities of Charity. They started in Châtillon in 1617, and then developed somewhat haphazardly. The greatest names of the French aristocracy were in them, from Louise-Marie de Gonzague, Queen of Poland, to the mother of the great Condé, from Baronness de Renty to Marshal Schomberg's wife, from the Duchess of Aiguillon to Madame de Pollalion, from Madame de Villeneuve to Madame de Miramion.

A pleasant little anecdote will show the sort of people involved. The Duchess of Nemours, mother of the great Condé, of the Prince de Conti and of the Duchess of Longueville, was grumbling in confession. The priest, a pious sort of man who had not been round much, asked her why; she said she could not forgive her three enemies. He asked her who they were and she said: The King of France, the King of Prussia and the Duke of Savoy.

Ladies like this were, in military terms, the General Staff of Vincent's initiatives. When he needed to get something new going it was to these he turned. He went over the idea with them, consulted them, exhorted them and then trusted them. They never let him down.

The Daughters of Charity were the second group. The whole thing began by chance, which was normal for Vincent. By 1623

Louise de Marillac was a woman at the end of her tether, directionless in her life. Her calvary, though, had begun long before. Right from her infancy she had lived at home like Cinderella, supported but unloved. She was born illegitimately in the Marillac household in 1591 and experienced neither warmth nor affection. Early on she was sent to the royal convent of the Dominican nuns in Poissy, as family members wished her to be kept out of sight. After that she was a lodger with a lady, though this was a worsening of her situation as Louise had to help out by working. Separated from her family she had the opportunity of maturing, with her spiritual life deepening; she prayed and read.

By then she had arrived at the time in life for making important decisions. She asked to be accepted into the Franciscan Daughters of the Passion, but the Capuchin Provincial, Fr Honoré de Champigny, did not think she was making the right decision; he told her her health was not up to it.

And so it looked as though after the door of her family house had been shut in her face now the door of God's house also was being closed to her. Marriage was the obvious solution, so her family arranged one and she became the wife of Antoine le Gras. The words "equerry and secretary", describing his position, don't really tell us very much. We are told more by the fact that Louise would be called "Mademoiselle" rather than "Madame", as this indicated an inferior social rank, that she was someone who did not count for much. They got married and nine months later had a son, Michel. Their married life was not happy. In a letter to Vincent later on in life she said that her husband had spent his life looking after the interests of others rather than those of his wife and son (I 345). He was constantly ill and he did not live long. Her son was a source of disappointment to her. She took refuge in God and in spiritual directors. She went into a dark tunnel, lit neither by the light of God nor of men. She asked the advice of Jean-Pierre Camus, the bishop of Belley. The bishop very wisely forbade her to go back over the past, thinking of what she had not been. The most he allowed her to do was to make a vow to remain a widow should she outlive her husband.

41

Then came Ascension Thursday 1623 and her darkness became even more dense; she wondered whether she should leave her husband, and was in a state of panic because her spiritual director was not available. She experienced the abandonment which Christ felt on the cross. When everything seemed just death and desolation there came an unexpected brilliant light. This happened at Pentecost, June 4, 1623, when Louise was in her parish church of St Nicolas des Champs in the rue Saint-Martin. While she was praying, or attending mass, an interior voice told her to stay with her husband because the time would come when she would be part of a community dedicated to the service of the poor. She did not understand how this could happen, given that she saw the sisters "going and coming". A clear assurance came to her that she would find a spiritual director, and God let her see him, and instead of being pleased with him she felt repugnance: it was Vincent.

The most likely reason for her not being pleased was that she did not see him as a priest matching her image of a great spiritual figure, with eyes raised to heaven and uttering weighty thoughts. He was a man who kept his eyes fixed on earth, being both realistic and humble. Vincent had no liking for manufacturing spiritual literature.

When he got to know Louise, in 1624 or 1625, he gave her clear, simple, directions. After her husband's death, on 21 December 1625, he was the anchor which saved her from being wrecked. Should she stop receiving communion, through a sort of distaste? Vincent told her that her life of faith could not be nourished by distancing herself from God: "Our Lord is continual communion for those who are united in both what he wills and does not will" (I 233). He advised her to ease up on her overdone spiritual practices in her prayer life: "God is love and wants us to go to him through love" (I 86). He taught her to avoid haste and to trust in God's providence which is to be followed and not overtaken (I 68). He showed her the importance of humility: "It is a single beautiful diamond, more valuable than a mountain of jewels" (I 82).

The years 1625 to 1629 are what writers call her years of widowhood. In 1629 there came a change. Not because she re-married, but because her life took on a new direction. She had told Vincent that she felt inclined to give herself to the poor (I 51). She began to visit the confraternities of charity. This meant that she had to get out of Paris, but also out of herself.

It was through visiting the confraternities that Louise noticed that there was something missing in the way the ladies gave their services. They were committed, they gave their time, devotion and care. They gave something, they gave a lot, but they did not give everything; they did not give over their entire life to this. What was needed was people who would give themselves fulltime to the service of the poor. She did not have to wait long to find some.

Generosity has its own irresistible appeal. That was what attracted Marguerite Naseau. Poverty forced her to tend cows, but she had free time and began to think. She wanted to do something more, and got the idea of teaching young people. She set about learning to read and write, all by herself. She bought an ABC and learnt four letters at a time. She was soon ready to teach others what she had learnt. She went to Vincent and he encouraged her to teach others. She had to put up with very great difficulties, but she was full of enthusiasm. When later on she heard that the sick poor were being cared for in Paris she took another step forward. She became the soul of the confraternity in Saint-Sauveur parish, and other girls followed her example. She died on the job. She had taken in a girl with the plague, and they slept in the same room. She was infected and her life was cut off like a flower. But the plant did not die. The little group was taken over by Vincent and passed on by him to Louise.

In the talk he gave on 5 July 1640, he outlined the plan of the vocation of the Daughters of Charity. The sisters are modelled on the Son of God who was called "to work for the neighbour, visiting and healing the sick, teaching the ignorant for their salvation" (IX

15). A fortnight later, on the 19th, he had the sisters together again and suggested as a subject for discussion the love for their vocation and the service of the poor. He contrasted their community with the Capuchins, the Carthusians and the Jesuits. The first had been raised up in order to honour God by poverty, the second by silence and the praise of God, and the Society of Jesus by an apostolic life. The poor girls "with the headgear" had the special purpose of serving the sick poor both corporally and spiritually (IX 19ff).

Some years later, on 13 February 1646, he reminded his sisters that from all eternity God had wanted them for the service of the poor (IX 242). And he added:

> In the past there were plenty of religious orders; there were plenty of hospitals founded for helping the sick; there were plenty of devoted nuns to serve them; but up to now no one ever saw the sick being cared for in their own rooms. If some member of a poor family fell ill the husband had to be separated from his wife, the wife from her children, the father from his family. Up to now, my God, you did not appoint any order to help them; and it seemed as if your adorable providence, which leaves no one out, did not bother about them (IX 246).

It was not just a question of any old help. The soul of the visit is love, a love called on to show God's goodness towards the sick poor, regarding them as lords and masters (X 331-333).

In the Rules for the Daughters of Charity he presents the purpose of the Daughters of Charity as centred on "honouring Jesus Christ, serving him corporally and spiritually in the person of the poor, whether sick or children, whether prisoners or others who, through shame, were afraid of making their needs known." The environment, the locality, of this service is not a cloister or convent but the world. Their place, then, is where people's needs are, and not behind the protection of a convent grille.

They are to remind themselves that, although they are not nuns, since that state would not be suitable for the work of their vocation, nevertheless, since they are more exposed outside than nuns, usually having only the houses of the sick as their convent, a rented room as their cell, the parish church as their chapel, the city streets or hospital wards as their cloister, obedience as their enclosure, the fear of God as their grille, and holy modesty as their veil, they are obliged, because of this, to lead a life as virtuous as if they were professed in some religious order, and to behave anywhere in the world where they might be with as much recollection, purity of heart and body, detachment from created things, and edification as real nuns in the seclusion proper to their own convent.

That is a very brave passage. Previous Church law, in order to safeguard the integrity of the life of dedicatation and prayer, had erected imposing barriers around monasteries, making enclosure obligatory. It was unheard of to think of a women's community dedicated to a ministry of service. Those who thought it a good idea admitted that there was no previous example of such a thing. Service came first, even to the extent that, if necessary, helping the poor was to come before community spiritual exercises, in so far as this was "leaving God for God." But there was no question of just mere "activity." If service called for mobility, the "going and coming" which Louise had glimpsed ten years before, it also called for real living people. An objection from the administrators of the public hospital in Paris, the Hôtel-Dieu, also had to be answered; they said that what they wanted from the sisters in charge was not just the raising of their eyes and hands to God. They did not know Vincent. He wanted strong personalities, able to contemplate as well as to serve, to console, to help; to roll up their sleeves, but also to live in dialogue with God. Vincent wanted to safeguard chastity, but also safeguard total service. In no way could he conceal the world from their eyes, so he had to withdraw it from their hearts. For this reason he wanted control of the senses, close liaison with the sister in charge; she had to be told of the need to go to a house in order to visit a sick person. The sister was not to go alone to such a person, and she was to avoid areas normally regarded as having a bad reputation, as well as sick people known for unchastity.

In order to protect their vocation Vincent arranged for vows, private ones renewed each year. Up to the 18th century the Church did not recognise any religious vows which did not include enclosure. Vincent had to work out original and clever loopholes in order to by-pass these obstacles and keep his Daughters in the service of the poor. Again and again he used to insist that the Daughters of Charity needed more virtue than other sisters. In making a comparison with the Ursulines he added that they educated well-to-do girls in their convents while the Daughters of Charity are called to teach not just children but all the poor whom they meet or help. For this reason vows were geared to service: they took vows in order to serve the poor.

This is why the chapters of their rule call for the sisters to be in constant contact with the poor. Obedience was not just to their superiors but also to the Parish Priests in whose parishes they ministered, to hospital authorities and to doctors. Their main service was to Jesus Christ in the persons of the sick. They were to bring the food themselves, to care for the sick corporally and spiritually, and not pass this work on to others.

Their spiritual life filled out the day with prayer. Their timetable was tightly packed. They got up at four o'clock, then prayer, then a piece of bread for breakfast and then an exhausting day of service till they went to bed at a quarter past eight at night.

In the beginning only very small communities were envisaged, giving a structured presence in a particular area. This meant that in a village there were, besides the superior, one sister for the village school, but only for girls who were poor, and not for boys of any sort, and one sister for those who were sick in their own homes or in the local hospital. In the special rules for sisters who worked in parishes it was emphasised that they were to reflect on the meaning of their vocation, namely spiritual and corporal help. With regard to the first, they were to teach the acts of faith, hope and charity, explaining repentance and acceptance of God's will. They were to recommend the making of a good general confession, which was, for Vincent, the key element in a mission. In order that their special spiritual practices should not interfere with service they were to be careful to help everyone in the same way. They were to be especially careful not to omit even the smallest item when ministering to a sick person, thinking only of God. Since they were serving God they were not to pay any attention to whether they were greeted with praise or insult.

Their ministry was completely gratuitous, so the sisters were forbidden to accept even the smallest gift; they were to regard themselves as owing something to the poor. For this reason the service of the sick poor was to take precedence over everything else, even their spiritual exercises. They were not, however, to take anything to eat or drink in other people's houses, nor were they to keep watch with sick people all through the night.

The timetable for sisters who helped the sick in their own homes was slightly different from the general one. After their meditation they were to bring medicine to the sick and then go to Mass. After that they went to the lady whose turn it was to prepare the meals and collected the pot of food. The food was distributed from nine till eleven. After lunch they were to study the doctor's prescriptions and prepare the medicines to be brought to the sick, and return the pot to the lady who prepared the meals. Around six in the evening in winter, or eight in the summer, they finally closed the door.

Louise de Marillac was equally clear about service of the poor in their homes. In 1647 she wrote to Sister Turgis, asking her if she had sick people to visit, and she noted that down the country sisters often had different people three miles or more apart. For this reason it was an honour to wear clogs which, as with the poor, were their means of getting around; but they were also their means of becoming holy. With a dash of healthy realism she pointed out how service was helpful to one's spiritual life: "Remember the remorse you used to feel in places where you did not have enough to do." The picture of the village sisters' life was quite clear in Louise's mind: one sister was for the school and another for visiting the sick. For example, in Chars one sister, Marie, took charge of teaching while the other, Clementine, visited the sick in hospital or at home, though the other sister was not forbidden to do this as well.

Since God saves people by means of other people, Vincent thought it necessary that the poor be saved by poor people. Since God saved people through love, he regarded it as necessary to put charity in the foreground. Since God became incarnate in Jesus Christ by means of a woman, so Vincent thought it indispensable that the salvation of the poor should be by means of women. But not just any sort of women, but women who could reflect like a diamond the many facets of Mary's face. That is why the Daughter of Charity came into being, a daughter of God and a daughter of Mary.

CHAPTER VI

New frontiers for the young Gascon

1633 brought a further change of direction for Vincent, the third such change. He was already fifty-three, and the period of ambition had been left far behind. The period of establishing new foundations was also over. What happened now was that he was given new and pressing responsibilities. He did not seek them, nor did he need them. It was other people, society, who recognised his charism. It was others who had need of him. He was ready, because he was free; free to serve.

In the first place, he was free to serve the Church. He co-operated in the renewal of monasteries, which was badly needed. Some monasteries had lost their fervour and their credibility. Many, too many, members of religious orders used to pray without really believing in it, and just put up with their rules. Vincent said to one such man, who wanted to leave his monastery and go to one where monastic observance had been watered down: "It is not an order, but a disorder ... The monks are libertines and bad-tempered." Because of her scandalous behaviour a certain abbess had been locked up in a monastery. She appealed to Adrien Le Bon, former prior of St Lazare, to ask Vincent to be lenient on her. Le Bon, in view of his having handed over St Lazare to Vincent, thought he was due a favour. Vincent would not budge. He was even prepared to hand St Lazare back, but he would not do that sort of favour.

He backed various attempts at reform which were started in his time, for example that of the Benedictines of St Maur, of the

Canons Regular whose reform was initiated by his friend Alain de Solminihac, of the Order of Grandmont and of the Dominicans.

As well as what he had done about retreats and seminaries, there was something else he did for the up-grading of priests' lives which must be mentioned. "The Tuesday Conferences" got their name from the fact that, from 1633 onwards, a group of priests used to meet on Tuesdays in Paris. The meetings were chaired by Vincent, and after a period of prayer the priests shared their thoughts and convictions about what it meant to be a priest. Their interaction was mutually encouraging, and on leaving these meetings all felt re-charged with new zeal; well, almost all. The future Cardinal de Retz was the exception, the youngest of the de Gondi boys, known to Vincent since his infancy. His family had wanted him to be a priest so that he could become archbishop of Paris, a post handed down from uncle to nephew in the de Gondi family. Someone recommended him to Vincent, who suggested to him that he come to the Tuesday Conferences. He went to only a few. In his memoirs he recalls that Vincent told him that he hadn't too much devotion but was not far from the kingdom of God.

He was an exception. Many future bishops used to attend these conferences, but Vincent was on his guard against those who were ambitious. To make them live up to their words he demanded commitment from them, so they gave missions to the blind, to the mentally disturbed, to prostitutes, to galley-slaves held in the Tournelle prison in Paris, to beggars. There was also the well-known mission to the royal household of Louis XIII, during which the king placed France under the protection of Mary.

When Louis XIII died on 14 May 1643 power passed to his widow, Anne, who became regent because their son, Louis XIV, was a minor. (She was the daughter of Philip III of Spain but is known in history as Anne of Austria beacuse she was of the Habsburg family). In addition to her ministers she also wanted around her a group of trusted persons to sort out problems of a religious nature. This group was popularly known as the Council of Conscience. It was not a structured group but met whenever the queen regent or her prime minister, Cardinal Mazarin, summoned it. She wanted Vincent as a member.

This was a significant indication of how highly he was regarded. He was into the world of people of influence, people whom he used to refer to as being "at the top", but he did not lose his head; in fact his humility deepened. For as long as he could, he refused to use a carriage. Later on they forced him to use one when he was becoming too tired.

One day a lady came to him to ask a favour, and to improve her chances she mentioned that she had been a servant to his mother. We don't know what he did, but we do know what he said: "My good woman, you are taking me for someone else; my mother never had servants; in fact she was one herself." It is easy to understand why, when a flatterer addressed him as "Monsignor" he merely said: "I'm only a pig-keeper."

The appointment of bishops was always on the agenda for meetings of the Council of Conscience. According to the concordat of 1516, the king had the right to put forward names of persons to become bishops. The Holy See reserved to itself the right of granting or refusing approval.

It is easy to understand why Vincent was showered with recommendations, once it was known that he was one of those who made the decisions. There is a legend about a duchess, whose son's name was turned down for a vacant diocese, who threw a footstool at Vincent's head. But there were, in reality, more lively episodes.

In 1646, after the death of the bishop of Bayeux, the president of the *Parlement* (The High Court) came forward to campaign for his own son, Edouard. He approached the queen and Mazarin, and they agreed; that was the way things used to work. Vincent, however, knew that young Molé was not of the right calibre, and went to the president of the *Parlement* and asked him to withdraw his son's candidature. Such a thing was unheard of. Others would have rebelled, and have thrown Vincent out as a scandal-monger. Molé bided his time, as he knew Vincent was right, but there was nothing he could do about it. He was hoping that with the advice of shrewd counsellors he would not have made too many serious mistakes. After five years the whole matter was resolved by the death of Edouard Molé.

On another occasion a rather odd request came Vincent's way. A member of a religious order, well-known as a preacher, put forward his own name for appointment as a bishop. He said that keeping the rule of his order had worn him out and interfered with his work for the good of souls. When Vincent read this sort of stuff his eyes used to gleam. He replied to the learned priest in such a way that he would not be embarrassed, but with a dash of humour administered in measured doses, which is a masterpiece of charity:

> I have no doubt at all that Your Reverence would do wonders as a bishop, if you were called to that by God, but he has made it clear, by the great success he has given to your ministry and your administration, that he wants you in your present work and there is no indication that he wants to withdraw you from it. If his Providence was calling you to be a bishop he would not turn to yourself to suggest that you look for this; he would rather let it be known to those who have the right to nominate people for posts and honours in the Church, that they would choose you for this without yourself having to make any move at all. In that way your vocation would be flawless and certain. But there seems to be something blameworthy in your putting yourself forward ... And what's more, my Reverend Father, think of the wrong you would be doing to your holy order by depriving it of one of its main supports; you

uphold it and bring credit on it by your teaching and example! If you open this door you are making way for others to follow your example ... Take my word for it, you should give up the work of preaching for a while to build up your health. You still have a lot to give to God and to your order, which is one of the holiest and most edifying in the Church of Jesus Christ (IV 18ff).

Because of his membership of the Council of Conscience Vincent, without wanting to be, was drawn into politics, but he did not let this go to his head. In his place of influence he became the voice of those who had no voice. In the final third of his life his history becomes entwined with the French wars of the time. After a period of peace, at least with neighbouring countries, the boom of cannon and the roll of drums began again.

There had, of course, been episodes of internal conflict, fighting within the royal family, popular uprisings, revolts of the nobles, the fight against the Huguenots. But during the 1630s it was the same politics which both started wars and made them inevitable. It was a deliberate decision by the king and Richelieu and, from their point of view, the only one.

It began in 1632 with the invasion of Lorraine, followed by war in the north and east of France. Whole provinces were laid waste, towns and villages burnt, harvests destroyed or plundered, so that the monsters of famine and plague sprang up on the threatening horizon. There were cases of canibalism and of feeding on carrion. For many people death was a relief and a liberation. In this tragic situation Vincent was not like the priest in the parable who "passed by on the other side"; he became a "neighbour".

When word came in 1636 that the Spanish had reached Corbie, about ten miles east of Amiens, Vincent told his community: "This is a time for penance, because God is afflicting his people." And in order to show solidarity with the worst-off, he asked for real sacrifices from his community. For example, good bread disappeared from the tables for three or four years. That wasn't enough. News reaching him from the war zones spoke of death and desolation. He screwed up his courage and, somehere between 1639 and 1642, the exact date is not clear, he went to Richelieu: "Give us peace, have pity on us, give peace to France" were the pleas which rose from his heart. The cardinal apologised, but there was nothing he could do. That, at least, was the line he tried to take with Vincent, who was not to be put off with such official words. Everything was going well in Paris, but things were not the same down the country. Faced with a new situation, he felt personally called. Everyone was his brother.

Solidarity and love dictated his reaction. He called a meeting of all the people who could help him. The queen donated the bed and the hangings which had been used at Louis XIII's funeral. The Duchess of Aiguillon did the same, after the death of her uncle, Cardinal Richelieu. Others donated less, but in proportion to their resources their help was far more generous. Then he sent his missioners into the war zones. His plan was to make them fan out into the areas where the need was greatest. He sent them the donations which he received so that they could give help directly to the people, without any middlemen. One missioner died of exhaustion in Bar-le-Duc on 19 January 1640. Vincent's comment was: "He died the way I want to die, which is what I ask God for." When he heard that six or seven hundred poor people followed the coffin he was amazed. At once he sent another priest to take his place, but he also fell sick. When he recovered he wrote to Vincent: "I have recently provided clothing for at least two hundred and sixty poor people. But how much greater a number have I 're-clothed' with confession and communion; I counted more than eight hundred in a single month."

The situation was tragic in Metz. Every morning corpses, gnawed by wolves, were removed from the streets. The bishop, Henri de Bourbon, illegitimate son of Henri IV, had been merely tonsured in order to be able to receive the revenue of the diocese. He had no interest at all in the poor who were dying of hunger; they did not even enter his thoughts. The situation was the same in Verdun, where the bishop, François de Lorraine, married a baroness in 1661. It was Vincent who thought about the poor.

The war had spread, and engulfed other regions in flames. Vincent sent more priests and lay brothers to establish Confraternities of Charity in order to induce everyone to help him. He forwarded grain and clothing, but also seed and ploughs so that people could regain their dignity and remedy their needy situation through their own efforts. "We are sending something to help some poor people to sow a small bit of land. I mean the poorest, those who, without this help, would not be able to do this" (VII 387). In 1642 the town council of Luneville thanked him in these words: "It had seemed that Heaven had nothing but punishment for us. But then one of your priests arrived, loaded with help, and the seriousness of our plight was eased, and our hopes raised again". But even this was not enough: "In these unfortunate times we must borrow money in order to survive ourselves and to help the poor".

The state of emergency in Lorraine ended with the close of the Thirty Years War in 1648, but this was not the case elsewhere. The civil war known as the Fronde broke out, Frenchman against Frenchman, king against his people. It was a complex situation, involving jealousy, hatred of Mazarin, the defence of party interests. Vincent had friends in both camps, in Paris which was under siege, and in the queen's army. He made a courageous attempt at mediation.

On the fiercely cold night of 14 January 1649, Vincent and a lay-brother left Paris on horseback. The two suspicious dark figures were stopped by the townspeople in Clichy who were on guard. Someone recognised Vincent and they were allowed through. At Neuilly the Seine was swollen; it had already carried away the Tuileries bridge and flooded a lot of land. The river was breaching its banks, but the two riders risked crossing. They reached Saint-Germain-en-Laye by mid-morning. Vincent was granted an audience by the queen. He described the miserable state of Paris and suggested she should dismiss Mazarin. Vincent was not some-one who worked behind the scenes and stabbed people in the back, so he also secured an appointment with Mazarin: "Give up ... throw yourself into the sea so that the storm may be calmed". That was the Jonah solution, but Mazarin was not Jonah and he retained his position. A diplomat as shrewd as himself did not expect such advice, but he did not get annoyed nor did he punish Vincent. But he did drop him from the Council of Conscience.

There was no point in staying on at Court, so he pressed on, still on horseback, along roads in very poor condition and in very bad weather. When he was fording a river the horse fell under him and he was nearly trapped. He was rescued, and got accommodation in an inn. When he had recovered somewhat he started teaching catechism.

He resumed his journey, travelling up and down the west of France, and was also sick for a while. Then he returned to Paris in a carriage given by the Duchess of Aiguillon. The archbishop of Paris, to overcome his reluctance, ordered him to keep it and to make use of it.

Fresh crises awaited him. Even the countryside around Paris, known as the Ile de France, needed aid. After that it was the turn of Picardy and Champagne. St Lazare became, to an even greater extent, a sort of central agency for relief. Ten thousand people were fed at St Lazare, fifteen thousand in Paris. The poor were ever more and more Vincent's burden and his sorrow. When someone told him there was nothing left in the money-box he replied: "That's good news. Now we can show we trust God." He sent his missioners off to the devasted areas. In 1651 alone there were sixteen or eighteen of his men in Champagne. The town council of Rethel wrote these bitter but grateful words: "No one up to now, apart from Your Reverence and those whom you sent, has had any compassion on our misfortunes" (IV 200). Letters reached him which were full of anguish. People wrote to him saying that without him everyone would have died of hunger (IV 8). Another letter said: "We can see in the charity you practice the original sort of Christian devotion, because in the early Church the Christians had only one heart and ensured that there would not be any poor person among them who would be left without help and assistance" (IV 233).

In 1652 he made another attempt at mediation between the two opposing parties in the Fronde. Mazarin was inflexible, and would not hear of any clemency for the princes or the Frondists. On 16 August 1652 Vincent wrote a letter full of feeling to Pope Innocent X. He described the situation in France, with all the realism of someone who has seen and experienced all the conflict, setting out the divisions caused by the warring parties:

> The royal family is split by dissensions, people are grouped into opposing camps, towns and provinces are torn by civil war, villages, towns and cities are destroyed, ruined, burnt. Farmers have no hope of harvesting what they sowed and are no longer sowing anything for the following year. Soldiers commit all sorts of excesses and go unpunished. For their part, the ordinary people are exposed not only to robbery and brigandage, but also to murder and every sort of torture. In rural areas those who do not die by the sword almost all die of hunger. Priests are no more spared than others by the soldiers, and they are inhumanly and cruelly treated, tortured, and killed. Young women are raped, and even nuns are at risk from the soldiers' debauchery and fury. Churches are profaned, pillaged or destroyed. Those churches which remain standing are, for the most part, abandoned by their priests so that the people are more or less deprived of the sacraments, of Mass and of all other spiritual help. Finally, horrible to contemplate and even more so to relate, the most blessed sacrament of the body of the Lord is treated most shamefully, even by Catholics. In order to steal the sacred vessels the eucharist is thrown on the ground and walked upon (IV 455).

Reconciliation, though, was on the horizon. Everyone wanted it but the defeated did not have the courage to surrender and the victors were unwilling to show magnanimity. It was feared that the monarch wanted to press on with the war against Spain in the north in order to overcome the capital (IV 473). The young king, Louis XIV, facilitated things. He dismissed Mazarin and promised an amnesty. These two gestures won the population back to him and he persuaded the leaders of the Fronde to desist. On 28 October the king was reconciled with his people.

New appeals were coming from the north, where the war against Spain was still going on. So up there, also, Vincent set up help centres, "Charities," hospitals. The big break-through, though, was that he sent sisters. Up to then, having women on the battle field was simply unthinkable; women who followed the armies did so for totally different reasons. When he was sending some of them Vincent told them: "Men go to war to kill other men, and you are going to bring remedies for the evil they do there" (X 507). After the Battle of the Dunes, on 14 June 1658, in which Turenne defeated Condé and the Spanish, the queen asked for six sisters. Vincent could find only four, two of whom died shortly afterwards. Another sister went to Vincent and offered to go as a replacement for those who had died in the work (VII 233, X 548).

CHAPTER VII

Least among the least

A furtive shadowy figure gliding through the night towards the doors of churches or aristocratic mansions to retrieve abandoned infants is the picture which history has bequeathed to posterity. Such a picture is inaccurate, inaccurate because it does not go far enough. The reason why Vincent did not, in fact, come out from St Lazare at night was because it would have been difficult for one single person to be of any help to so many unfortunates. His greatness and his genius show in the fact that he aroused in others interest in, and commitment to, the poor. Many, both during his lifetime and afterwards, dedicated their lives to serving them, and in this they found their joy and fulfilment.

The span of his interest was broad and varied. He did not have to tire himself out going looking for the poor. He saw them, he sensed them. Every time he went out into the city his glance met that of a people abandoned by everyone. Or almost everyone; Vincent was always on their side. He had made a choice for life, and he wanted to stay on the side of the poor, not misty-eyed with compassion but with the spirit of someone who wanted to give back dignity and hope to these people. He did not want the poor to remain poor, any more than he looked on them as a way in which the wealthy could merit something for heaven. His idea was to enable them to escape from their poverty. In 1659 he wrote to one of the lay brothers of his community who was engaged in helping war-ravaged areas:

We would also like to see all the other poor people who

have no land earning their livelihood ... by giving farm implements to the men so that they can work, and spinning wheels and flax or wool to girls and women for spinning; this would be only for the poorest ones. Now that peace is here everyone will find something to do and the soldiers will no longer take what the people have, so they can get something together and gradually re-establish themselves ... and let them know that they must no longer expect any help from Paris (VIII 72-73).

Vincent was one of the spiritual masters who best understood the mystery of God and man. God intervenes in history to provoke us into coming out of ourselves and being opened up towards something other than ourselves. The face of God revealed in Jesus Christ is a face which always looks towards others. That is why Vincent, instead of gazing on the face of the Son of God, looked for human faces and loved them with an intense, burning, love. It is on record that Pierre de Bérulle spent each Trinity Sunday in total isolation so that he could "honour" the three Divine Persons in their eternal silent communion. In reflecting on Christ, Blaise Pascal, according to his *Mémorial*, saw not just "Jesus Christ" but also "disregard for the world". His picture is "catastrophic", being of a God who extinguishes signs, who speaks only through pain, who can be found only through annihilation in an undiluted surge of faith which does not try to discover the reason for this period of suffering which stretches between ourselves and the end of the world. Vincent, on the other hand, found his Lord through looking at the suffering crowds, the poor, the sick, the devasted regions, and in his Lord he found his brothers. He was fully conscious of the real condition of the poor, but they did not turn him off. He did not seek to disregard the world in order to find Jesus; he found him in the world which, even without being lit up by the thrilling hope of Teilhard de Chardin, and in spite of the muddiness of its furrows, always retains the hope of life.

There were many categories of poor to keep Vincent busy. First of all came the sick, both those who were laid up at home and those who were in hospital. In the case of the latter it was just around this time, the seventeenth century, that the hospital system was developing.

Vincent was acquainted with the sick and used to visit them. The Hôtel-Dieu, the Hôpital de la Charité, the Petites Maisons, St Louis, the Salpêtrière were places well known to him, and he found in them stricken people whose plight moved him to the very depths of his being. In the Hôtel-Dieu the wards were neither lit nor ventilated, and what people of the time noticed most was the appalling smell. The sick were not segregated according to their type of illness, but were all together in an unbelievable mass, several even being in the one bed. As soon as a place became vacant through the death of a patient another was immediately put there.

Geneviève Fayet, widow of Antoine Goussault, got the idea of inviting the Ladies of Charity to go to the Hôtel-Dieu, and Vincent backed her up in this. She became the inspiration of this group of Ladies, but she wanted to be called their "servant". Vincent's idea was that the Ladies would be visitors, not nurses. This was no new idea; helping the poor has always been a part of Christianity. Historical investigation into poverty has shown that in the Middle Ages there were always corporations or guilds whose purpose was to help the poor and the sick. Nowadays poverty is seen differently, with the traditional image of the poor person being transformed into a person who, from either the social or the sanitary point of view, is a source of danger. In hospitals in those days there could be found persons with all types of sickness: insanity, malaria, tuberculosis, heart disease, stomach or bladder trouble. In the face of such a sight people were bewildered. They reacted by either fleeing from it or behaving imprudently. Marguerite Naseau, traditionally called "the first Daughter of Charity", did the latter and brought on her own death by sharing her bed with a victim of the plague.

Service of the poor was, for Vincent, a supreme act of love, the sign of a real follower of the gospel. In 1650 Vincent wrote to one of his priests:

> I like very much your decision to continue to administer the sacraments to the sick, to give some sort of instruction in the hospital on feast-days and to teach catechism on Sundays, as is fitting for a true child of the gospel. But it would be even better if, in spite of the prohibition, you did not give up your visits to the sick. You used to visit them every day, consoling them in their troubles and encouraging them to be patient; keep this up, please. Teach prayers of resignation, love of God and trust in his mercy to some, and lead others towards sorrow and repentance. In other words, prepare them to die well if their illness is terminal, or to live well if God is going to leave them in this world still. This work, which goes on and on, is boring, of course, to those who do not realise how important it is. But to you, Father, who understand its worth and, thanks be to God, take the salvation of the poor to heart, it must bring untold consolation as well as happiness without compare. Up to now this charitable work of yours has helped thousands, bringing eternal life to ever so many who have passed through your hands. Lord God, Father, could there be anything in the world which could turn you away from, or even turn you against, a work so precious in the sight of God! Do you ever think of how many upper-class people in Paris, of both sexes, visit, instruct and encourage the patients in the Hôtel-Dieu every day, doing this work with admirable devotion, not to mention perseverance? Of course, those who have not seen this find it hard to believe, while those who have seen it are greatly edified because, in reality, this visiting is the way saints live, great saints, serving our Lord in his members and in the best possible way (IV 84).

This, being such a sublime commitment, called for lots of courage to undertake it. Around 1632-33 Vincent wrote to Louise de Marillac about the plague:

God's goodness towards those who dedicate themselves to him in the Confraternity of Charity, no member of which ever caught the plague, gives me absolutely perfect confidence that you will come to no harm. Would you believe, Mademoiselle, that not only did I visit the late sub-prior of St Lazare, who was dying of the plague, but that I felt his breath? In spite of this neither I nor the others who helped him right up to the end were infected (I 185).

As regards actual hospital work, we must remember that the first hospital taken on by Vincent for the Daughters of Charity was the one in Angers, in 1640. The problems which arose in the hospitals were by no means insignificant. The local administration had a determining role, and this could cause conflict with the central administration of the community. The influence of the Ladies of Charity, with whom the Daughters had close links in the beginning, was pretty well wiped out. For this reason, Vincent and Louise had to insist on precisely-worded clauses being included in contracts, as happened in Angers, St Denis (1645), Nantes (1646) and Montreuil-sur-Mer (1647). Right up to 1668 the central administration of the Daughters of Charity was reluctant to take on hospitals, though later on this became the characteristic and normal work of the community. In the period just before the French Revolution the Daughters were in charge of 175 hospitals in France. In 1658 Louise de Marillac wrote to Brother Bertrand Ducournau, Vincent's secretary:

> You must make the young girls of Saint-Fargeau, who are asking to be accepted into the company of the Daughters of Charity, realise that this is not a religious order, even less a hospital from which they will never come out, but that the vocation calls for them to go looking for the sick poor in all sorts of places, no matter what the weather is like.

The poor had to be directly served by the Daughters. The one appointed to receive the sick was to consider herself as their servant, and to consider them as her lords and masters. In this spirit she will wash their feet with hot water, de-louse them and cut their hair if necessary, change their shirts and give them a little white cap or other covering for the head, then put them to bed, having first warmed the bedclothes to be given them, and give them hot soup and a drinking cup.

Great love was shown towards all the poor, but not always in exactly the same proportions. Vincent had preferences, especially for abandoned infants and the mentally deranged. On feastdays there was a large basket to the left of the main door of Notre-Dame which was full of infants, cared for by nurses who asked people to take charge of the babies. This was a touching sight, but it did not solve the problem. Rather more was done by a public institution called La Couche, but it was quite incapable of coping with the demands of so many defenceless beings. Many died, some were taken by pitiless beggars who maimed them and forced these poor creatures to beg. Neither personal care nor tenderness was shown to them, and a frightening percentage of them died.

Vincent tackled this problem and came up against certain difficulties. The Ladies of Charity were not in agreement about taking on such work, speculating that it might encourage immorality. Besides, the work entailed enormous expense; weren't there more urgent needs? Perhaps they thought it was going too far to give time to creatures who "were of no use". The work, however, made a start in 1638, with few children at first but the numbers quickly increased. Two years later Vincent decided to take the work over completely and, in January 1640, called a meeting of the Ladies. The greatest names in France were represented at it, but they were not discussing either clothes or jewellery, they were not criticising hair-dos or people. Their eyes were expectant, and they held their breath, hoping that Vincent would call a halt to this work, but in their hearts they knew they were deluding themselves.

Vincent's words came straight from the heart. He did not think in terms of resources, but of the need: to refuse to help was the same as killing the infants. Oddly enough, none of them felt stingy, because Vincent knew how to keep them on his side. They felt they were championing a cause and they committed themselves. The Daughters of Charity did the same. In a fatherly talk to them he let them see the nobility of their work for abandoned infants:

> If ordinary people regard it as an honour to serve the children of important families, you should think yourselves even more honoured in being called to serve God's children (IX 132).

He went on to say that in the ordinary course of events his listeners might have become mothers of children of their own, and if they had been employed in important households their wages would not have been very high,

> but what will you receive for having served these infants, who were abandoned by the world? God, for all eternity (IX 136).

Vincent, being a realist, knew how to keep an account of his work. In the first five years of their existence, the Daughters had helped about 1,200 infants. He had received donations, but not anything like enough. Some over-cautious people began to suggest that it was tempting Providence; it was too much, and should not be kept up. But Vincent did not see it like that. In 1647 he gave another of his famous talks, reported by Abelly, his first biographer, in 1664. He went carefully through the pros and cons and ended up:

> So, Ladies, compassion and charity led you to adopt these little creatures as your children. Since those who were their mothers by nature abandoned them you became their mothers by grace. Just for a moment, stop being their mothers and become their judges, with the power of life or death for them in your hands. I'm going to have a poll and check votes, as it is time to pass sentence and find out

whether you no longer intend showing them mercy. They will live if you continue your charitable help for their upkeep. On the other hand, if you give them up they will certainly perish and die; experience tells you that there is no doubt about that.

In 1649 the civil war known as the Fronde dried up many of his sources of income. Some nurses brought back the children because they had not been paid by the Ladies. There were shortages of bread, clothing and money. The only thing they were not short of was debt. So Vincent decided to call one more meeting of the Ladies of Charity. Many of them said they had no money left. But they had jewellery, possessions, valuable paintings, colourful tapestries, gowns and servants. And, not for the first time, Vincent succeeded in persuading them.

Vincent also had a predilection for the mentally ill. The gospel is a sort of madness, the folly of the Son of God, the scandal and insanity of the Cross. For Vincent the white cloak which Herod threw over Christ was a prophetic gesture, indicating that even the mentally unbalanced were not debarred from grace. And he wanted to have such people near him, in St Lazare. In 1655 he sent some Daughters of Charity to the Hospice des Ménages to help these most innocent of all detained persons.

His charity towards detained persons who were guilty also began very early. In a certain sense he learnt his trade with the galley-slaves. He used to be very scared going to where they were imprisoned. He set his mind to work on the logistical problems and succeeded in getting the galley-slaves transferred to La Tournelle prison in Paris, and also supported the idea of a hospital for them in Marseilles. The main force behind this latter project was the saintly bishop Jean-Baptiste Gault who died in 1643, happy to have picked up his fatal illness on the galleys and to die "in a real bed of honour". In 1640 Vincent sent a group of the Daughters to this hospital. This was an absolutely unheard of thing, especially when we recall that Vincent had many times protested against the admission of prostitutes. But when he understood the importance of feminine tenderness in this ministry he did not think twice about it. He recommended the Daughters to be humble, circumspect, prudent; he suggested that they look on themselves as the three young men in the fiery furnace in the book of Daniel. He had seen the galley-slaves treated like animals; the Daughters were the right people to go and serve them because "when we say Daughters of Charity we are saying Daughters of God".

This was the background to Barbe Angiboust's heroism. She was often treated badly: she had her heavy pot of hot soup spilt all over her, she was insulted with foul language, but she said nothing, gathered up everything and forgave them. Many times she stopped the warders from beating up the prisoners.

The problem of beggars was another matter which Vincent looked into. This was both a scourge and a provocation. As a scourge it bothered the middle of the road ordinary people; they would not put up with the number, the vice, the crudity of the poor. So, although in the Middle Ages people lived side by side with the poor, even to the extent of thinking of them as a blessing, from the 16th century onwards beggary became the synonym for immorality, a condition for which the poor had only themselves to blame; no one bothered to investigate the causes of their condition. Almsgiving was still allowed, but as the lesser evil.

In the 17th century came the idea of solving the problem of beggars by rounding them up; this meant driving them off the streets and getting them to work, an idea stemming from a profit-making mentality.

In 1653, at the end of the Fronde, Vincent met someone who gave him a very large sum of money, about 100,000 *livres*, for his charitable work; this donor wished to remain anonymous. He bought a house with a signboard of "The Name of Jesus" and had it converted to accommodate forty residents, twenty men and twenty women. These residents were comfortably lodged, with the possibility of working, free from worries and living in a religious atmosphere. This fitted in perfectly with Vincent's idea of helping people both corporally and spiritually.

The Ladies of Charity, seeing the good results of "The Name of Jesus," which was outside the walls of Paris near St Lazare, thought of suggesting a similar establishment inside the city and they asked Vincent to inaugurate it. In their minds this was to be the solution to the problem of beggars. They got down to work. Louise de Marillac was of the opinion that the political solution was the main idea behind this work and that therefore it should be entrusted to men; had the idea of charity been to the forefront it would be better to let women run it.

The Queen of France, Anne of Austria, was in favour of the scheme. Vincent was the only person who was hesitant. He excused himself with the plea that Noah spent a hundred years building the ark. He suggested making an experiment with one or two hundred poor people:

> Let's accept only those who volunteer to come, not putting pressure on anyone; if these are well treated and happy they will attract others; in that way, little by little, the numbers will build up with the resources which Providence will provide. Nothing will be spoilt by that way of acting; on the other hand, haste and pressure interfere with God's plan.

When the royal edict prohibiting begging was proclaimed in March it had precisely the effect Vincent had forseen. Those who refused to conform were treated too drastically. Vagabonds, outcasts and all beggars from the provinces were hunted. Panic resulted when bands of archers were seen at street corners hunting beggars. There were 40,000 beggars in Paris and only one tenth of these obeyed the edict.

Vincent looked on this round-up as a police action. The community in St Lazare had been appointed chaplains to look after the salvation of the poor, with the role of superiors but under the hospital administration. Vincent and his community refused to agree to such a proposal. He did not want to get involved in a solution to the problem of beggars which was profit-motivated and backed up by police action. He turned down the appointment, although it was proposed by the Ladies. He had too much respect for the poor to become their jailer.

CHAPTER VIII
Overseas

Everyone has a weak point: money, sex, power, ambition. Vincent's weak point was the poor. He expended all his energy on them; he discovered new resources and increased vocations. He had known how to say "no" to the queen when she had wanted to put him in charge of the ambiguous plan known as the General Hospital, mentioned at the end of the last chapter. But he was unable to refuse the appeal from the slaves in Tunis and Algiers, nor that from Madagascar.

His reason for sending his missioners across the Mediterranean to Tunis and Algiers was to cater for the needs of Christians held as slaves in Algeria and Tunisia, about 20,000 in the former and 6,000 in the latter. This slave population was the equivalent of the combined population of two medium-sized towns at the time, say Grenoble which did not reach 20,000 till 1710 and Nancy which, in 1645, had between four and five thousand.

There was no problem about going to Islamic areas for anyone who wanted to, but staying there was another matter. Vincent, shrewd man that he was, looked for diplomatic exemption for his missioners' activity. One possibility was open to him, an acceptable practice at that time, namely the purchase of certain appointments. This system worked, as the concept of the State was different then from now. The Duchess of Aiguillon helped him by buying the right to appoint consuls to Algiers and Tunis.

One of Vincent's priests, Julien Guerin, landed in Tunis in November 1645 to present his credentials as consul. He began by keeping his eyes open and behaving very circumspectly. He had a low-profile opening of a chapel and began celebrations open to the public. At Easter 1647 he obtained authorisation to spend ten days catechising the slaves on board one galley. In the meantime the consulate in Algiers was also established.

A lot of things were going on in these two centres, and diplomatic credentials did not count for much. The consul in Algiers was beaten up, imprisoned and forced to pay debts contracted by Christians who had either gone bankrupt or fled.

Diplomatic immunity was relative, sanitary immunity was non-existent, and the fact of the matter is that the Vincentian presence in Africa was dotted with courageous deaths. The plague began its harvest by reaping the life of Boniface Nouelly in 1647 in Algiers. Jacques Lesage and Jean Dieppe died shortly after this. Julien Guerin's turn came in 1648 in Tunis, whilst Jean Le Vacher managed to survive.

Those who replaced them had to be careful, as Vincent warned Jean Le Vacher and his brother Philippe. They were to visit the slaves and give them time and effort in solving their problems, comforting them and catechising them, overcoming distrust and danger. The whole matter was further complicated when there was question of trying to win back apostates. Pedro Bouruny, a young Balearic Christian, was threatened with appalling torture. His remorse at having apostatised tormented him interiorly, and he kept repeating: "Christ died for me so it is just that I should die for him." Having made up his mind to return to the Christian faith he went to the Pasha and said so. All this achieved was to make his death certain. A pyre was lit and this young martyr was transformed into that lamp which is put on the lampstand, and not hidden under a tub.

On hearing this Vincent was full of admiration for his missioners. Years later he spoke to his community in St Lazare about zeal:

> Zeal ... is made up of a genuine desire to please God and to be useful to others; zeal for extending God's kingdom, zeal for achieving others' salvation; is there anything in the whole world more perfect than this? If God's love is fire, then zeal is its flame; if God's love is a sun, zeal is its ray. Zeal is the purest element in loving God (XII 307-8).

The other overseas expansion was to Madagascar. What was the point in sending his men down to that latitude, to an unhealthy island below the tropic of Capricorn? Why face up to such a long journey – it took from five to nine months – why incur huge expense and put human lives at risk? The answer is to be found in a passion for the gospel, in the fire which interiorly consumed him, which is the mainspring of saints. One day he told his community:

> Risking your life is a sort of martyrdom, going overseas just for the love of God and the salvation of others (XI 423).

The whole thing started with an initial group of missioners sent to Madagascar in 1648. Their brief was to be Christian ministers for the French colonists and to evangelise the Malagasy people. All told, the number of missioners which Vincent sent over the years came to twenty-five.

As soon as the missioners arrived in Fort Dauphin, at one end of the big island, they began their apostolic work. One of them died almost immediately, but Charles Nacquart started straight in to work with the local inhabitants. He administered only a few baptisms but preached the gospel to large numbers. His idea was to build this young Christian enclave on the rock of solid convictions rather than on a large numerical total of converts. Among his many plans was a projected catechism in the Malagasy language. He asked Vincent for help.

Four years after the first group left, a second one set out. Their superior was a man who had been regarded as rather insignificant in France, Toussaint Bourdaise, but who was on fire with apostolic zeal. Before reaching Madagascar one of the priests in the group died. When they landed Fr Nacquart was not there to greet them; he had died four years previously. Two more of Bourdaise's companions also died. He wrote a letter of great sadness to Vincent:

> Fr Bellville ... died on the voyage, Fr Prevost ...has died, Fr Dufour ... has died ... I am the wretched servant who has been left to tell you the tale (VI 195).

Vincent sent yet another expedition in 1656, but this ended before it had even started, as the ship was wrecked while still in the River Loire. What Vincent found hardest to put up with was the lack of news; his men were far away and he knew nothing about how they were. He prayed and hoped. When a ship arrived in Nantes in the summer of 1657 he told his community about it:

> We know that a boat has reached Nantes, but as no news has come we are still waiting to find out something about our distant confreres. Are they dead? Are they alive? We don't know. No matter what state they are in, let's pray to God for them. And even if it's true that they are dead, should we, for that reason, abandon this work, this land which they and their predecessors had begun to reclaim? Oh, Jesus, we must be on our guard against such an idea (XI 411).

The following year he was thinking about another expedition, but this ended by the ship being captured by a Spanish vessel. In a talk to his community on 11 November 1658, he passed on to them, in a voice choked with emotion, the succession of news items which was bombarding him: The plague was getting worse in Warsaw; in the previous year it had claimed all the community in Genoa. The consulates in North Africa were in danger. Missioners were in constant danger while travelling. When he got that far he gave a sort of start, remembering suddenly that Fr Bourdaise was living by himself in Madagascar:

Fr Bourdaise, my brothers, let's pray for Fr Bourdaise who is so far away and all by himself and who, as you already know, has brought to birth for Jesus Christ, with so much trouble and care, a great number of the poor people of the country where he is. Fr Bourdaise, are you still alive or not? If you are, may it please God to preserve your life! If you are in heaven, pray for us! (XII 67).

In fact Bourdaise had died more than eighteen months previously. A further expedition was also shipwrecked, and returned to France.

CHAPTER IX

Unless the seed dies

There are two ways of looking at Vincent. The first looks at him from the outside, like the few portraits of him which exist. His expression is relaxed, he has a moustache and a not very thick beard flecked with grey, and two marvellous eyes, gentle and luminous, but also penetrating.

But there is another way of looking at him, from the inside as it were, as we go through his letters and his life. We see him as a real man, humble but not defeatist, gentle but not weak, simple and opposed to pointless complexity, but not superficial.

He was a man of action, to a remarkable degree. He often used to tell himself, according to his first biographer: "You have not earned the bread you are eating." His daily workload was frightening. His duties as Superior General of two communities, his role with the Ladies of Charity, all the requests which came to him from the royal court, the advice which important people looked for from him, the needs of the poor, the more than 30,000 letters which he wrote or dictated, the organisational demands of his charitable work, all these ate into his time or, in fact, consumed it on him. That is why he did not feel himself getting old; he simply did not have the time to think about it or to lament it.

In spite of such a pace of life he was not tense, off-putting or frantic. Although he was an organisational genius it is the spirit of his work which strikes us and not just the technique. He was conscious of carrying out God's work.

The things of God get done in their own way and real wisdom means following Providence step by step (II 473).

He followed, without fuss. This meant that he was slow to take initiatives. But when he discerned signs of God's will in some work, he became determined, firm and unshakable.

What is the secret of this? The answer is: prayer. Vincent's spiritual life does not, on the one hand, lean towards fleeing from the world nor, on the other, towards a purely political programme, a mere anti-hunger campaign. He did not coin the catch-phrase that you can't speak of God to an empty stomach. That notion comes from someone with less of both a sense of God and respect for the individual. Vincent regarded both needs as equally compelling. It is not his way to think in terms of primary and secondary; a person is in danger as soon as he is in either material or spiritual poverty.

Vincent answered the objections of one of his priests, who found it odd that the burden of hospital work should be taken on as well as that of giving missions, by a series of questions:

> But why, someone will say, should we take on the burden of a hospital? ... When priests give themselves to caring for the poor they do the same work as our Lord and many great saints ... Aren't the poor the suffering members of our Lord? Aren't they our brothers? If priests abandon them who do you want to look after them? So if there were someone among you who thought of belonging to the Congregation of the Mission just to evangelise the poor and not to help them, to provide for their spiritual needs but not their material ones, I answer such a person that we have to help them and get help for them in every way ... That is to evangelise them by word and deed (XII 87).

It was the coupling of charity and the gospel which brought about the link between his thinking and his activity. He would never have gone for the idea of holiness as mere human development, because that would have excluded the idea of charity.

Where did his sense of God come from? From his humility. Everyone knows how much it meant to him. He did not baulk at opposing Mazarin. It is said that the Queen of France, Anne of Austria, actually suggested he be made a cardinal. He dealt with prominent people as equal to equal. Yet he had a humility we find it hard to understand. He used to belittle himself. He referred to himself as worse than the devil, as a sinner, an ignoramus, a former pig-keeper. In 1642 he wanted to resign as Superior General. He wanted his missioners to have the same attitude. If they went to a meeting they were to take the lowest place. He himself and his missioners were to think of themselves as baggage handlers for the older and stronger religious communities. Such humility is not the result of metaphysical reflection but springs from the life-experience of someone who has discerned that God has sought him out and drawn him to himself. If a God left the ninety-nine sheep in safety to go and look for the one which had strayed and got separated from the flock, it meant that he, Vincent, was important in God's eyes. This impressed him. He felt he was loved, so he wanted to love. This reaction developed through his zeal, his passion for souls. He once admitted:

> Old and decrepit as I am, I must not fall off in my readiness to go to the Indies to win souls for God.

Humility, a shrewd humility, taught him not to look at facts and persons with rose-tinted spectacles. He had a sense of humour, but not in the form of pulling someone's leg. He had, rather, a nice way of deflating people with an exaggerated opinion of their own importance. He congratulated one of his priests, a Frenchman, who, after being in Italy for some time, was able to say "Signor, si." He told of a group of his missioners who had been shipwrecked and had experienced a shortage of food but who were once again safe "and with healthy appetites". A member of a religious order, who fancied himself as suitable to be appointed a bishop, was told to leave the evaluation of his talents to the judgement of others, and that a short rest was a good antidote to pride. A superior complained that members of his community were sick, and Vincent replied that three were worth ten when God took a hand. This was a nice way of recalling that salvation comes from God; it is his job, not ours. On one occasion a Parish Priest contacted Vincent about a priest who was looking for a position as curate. This man had once been in the Congregation of the Mission, but had left; then he re-joined but left a second time. Vincent replied to the Parish Priest that he did not know the man in question well "although he left our community twice" (VII 495).

One result of his humility was an out-of-the-ordinary charity, revealed in wonderful gentleness. Precisely because he had real humility he could bend down to human misery and relieve it. Speaking once about the galley-slaves he said: "If I kissed their chains ... they listened to me."

He did not like problems or problem-people: "The more we stare at the sun the less we see." That is why he was not cut out to get along with Jansenists. These were enthusiasts for an interpretation of St Augustine's theology as expounded mainly by two champions, Cornelius Jansen ("Jansenius" in Latin) and Jean Duvergier de Hauranne, usually known as the Abbé de Saint-Cyran. In France the Jansenist party was centred on Port Royal, an abbey of Cistercian nuns not far from Paris. They took as their standpoint a biased interpretation of the state of the Church at that time and wanted to reform it as regards morals, liturgy and discipline in a radical way, a very questionable way.

Vincent had been a friend of Saint-Cyran, so he knew his man. He really had no stomach for his constant criticism of the Church and he did not think that the way to re-evangelise Europe involved preaching a Christ who had not died for everybody, and a human condition so intrinsically ruined by sin that every human act not motivated by grace was an additional reason for damnation.

Vincent knew that Richelieu had more than one reason for dissenting from Saint-Cyran. He feared him as a political opponent, but also because of his influential teaching which could affect the balance of power. In 1638 the all-powerful cardinal had Saint-Cyran arrested and started a court case against him. If he had succeeded in getting evidence against the teaching of the accused from people like Vincent he would have had Saint-Cyran where he wanted him. Vincent was summoned to give evidence. On the one hand he knew that plenty of blame attached to Saint-Cyran, but, on the other, he had no wish to play the cardinal's purely political game. At that time it was not the teaching of the Church which was at stake, but only a power struggle. Vincent therefore gave his evidence so adroitly that no basis for accusation could be drawn from it. One biographer called it "a masterpiece of charity".

What he did for Saint-Cyran was not done through fear. When the Jansenist trouble broke out shortly afterwards, Vincent saw his responsibilities clearly and joined those who petitioned the Pope for the condemnation of Jansenius' most important book, *Augustinus*. He then set himself to limit the Jansenist infection and preserve his two communities from it. His activity was in harmony with the bishops and some of the most influential people in the Church in France, people like Condren, Olier and Eudes. In contrast to the anti-Jansenism of the politicians (Richelieu, Mazarin, Louis XIV) and of the theologians, the opposition of these "spiritual leaders" was not from the dogmatic-moral angle nor from that of being against the international politics of the two cardinal ministers. What was at stake was love for the Church and the salvation of the ordinary people. Vincent, along with Condren, Olier and Eudes, could not accept that one individual theologian could, through pride, proclaim himself as the reformer of the Church. Nor could he accept what was even worse, that the suffering people of the 17th century should have preached to them the idea of a stern God who did not die for everyone, instead of a merciful one. Hearing a theologian preach that a person could not be saved who did not understand the mysteries of the Trinity and Incarnation, Vincent commented:

"I'm afraid of being damned because I have not uninterruptedly devoted myself to teaching the poor people." For him the hope of the poor was the image of a benevolent and merciful God. He could not therefore leave them on their own, exposed to preaching which was stern and off-putting.

Vincent lived on to an advanced age. One gets the impression that his holding on to life and the slowing down of his aging process were due to his reluctance to give up a commitment to service. He wanted to remain at his post right up to the end.

During 1659 his health deteriorated. There came a time when he could not leave St Lazare, his headquarters, except in a carriage. In 1660 he had to be content with saying mass in the infirmary. His condition was visibly worsening. He was in pain and could not sleep, which led to daytime drowsiness. For him it was a sign that the brother, sleep, was giving advance notice of the arrival of the sister, death.

On Sunday 26 September 1660 he received the last sacraments. That night he was watched over by members of his community who repeated prayers and ejaculations, which Vincent joined in or answered less and less as the night progressed; his last word was "Jesus". He died at 5.45 on the morning of Monday, 27 September, sitting in a chair fully clothed, at the fireside, as if ready to set out on a long journey.